T0334141

Cambridge Elements ⹀

Elements on Women in the History of Philosophy
edited by
Jacqueline Broad
Monash University

OLYMPE DE GOUGES

Sandrine Bergès
Bilkent University

CAMBRIDGE
UNIVERSITY PRESS

CAMBRIDGE
UNIVERSITY PRESS

University Printing House, Cambridge CB2 8BS, United Kingdom

One Liberty Plaza, 20th Floor, New York, NY 10006, USA

477 Williamstown Road, Port Melbourne, VIC 3207, Australia

314–321, 3rd Floor, Plot 3, Splendor Forum, Jasola District Centre,
New Delhi – 110025, India

103 Penang Road, #05–06/07, Visioncrest Commercial, Singapore 238467

Cambridge University Press is part of the University of Cambridge.

It furthers the University's mission by disseminating knowledge in the pursuit of
education, learning, and research at the highest international levels of excellence.

www.cambridge.org
Information on this title: www.cambridge.org/9781009010528
DOI: 10.1017/9781009023702

© Sandrine Bergès 2022

This publication is in copyright. Subject to statutory exception
and to the provisions of relevant collective licensing agreements,
no reproduction of any part may take place without the written
permission of Cambridge University Press.

First published 2022

A catalogue record for this publication is available from the British Library.

ISBN 978-1-009-01052-8 Paperback
ISSN 2634-4645 (online)
ISSN 2634-4637 (print)

Cambridge University Press has no responsibility for the persistence or accuracy of
URLs for external or third-party internet websites referred to in this publication
and does not guarantee that any content on such websites is, or will remain,
accurate or appropriate.

Olympe de Gouges

Elements on Women in the History of Philosophy

DOI: 10.1017/9781009023702
First published online: July 2022

Sandrine Bergès
Bilkent University

Author for correspondence: Sandrine Bergès, sandrineberges@gmail.com

Abstract: Olympe de Gouges, though a well-known historical figure, has not been investigated as a philosopher until quite recently. Yet many of her writings have philosophical import, whether they are written in the genre of the philosophical treatise, drama, or political pamphlets. In the three main sections, the author gives an overview of some of Gouges's arguments, showing their originality and their relevance to debates contemporary to her and to us. In the Introduction, the author addresses the question of genre and argues that Gouges should be read as a philosopher, as well as a playwright and political writer. In the final section, the author draws out the relevance of her work for contemporary philosophers.

Keywords: Gouges, revolution, women's rights, slavery, republicanism

© Sandrine Bergès 2022

ISBNs: 9781009010528 (PB), 9781009023702 (OC)
ISSNs: 2634-4645 (online), 2634-4637 (print)

Contents

1 Introduction

1.1 Becoming Olympe de Gouges

Olympe de Gouges was born Marie Gouze in 1748 in Montauban, in the Tarn-et-Garonne, a region of France also known as Occitany.[1] Before the Revolution, when Paris asserted its cultural supremacy over the rest of the country, French was not the principal language spoken in Montauban. Instead, Marie would have been brought up speaking Occitan, or Languedoc, as well as a heavily accented French which would have set her apart when she moved to Paris in her twenties. Her mother was Anne-Olympe Mouisset, daughter of a well-respected solicitor and textile merchant. The Mouisset family had close ties with the local gentry, the Le Franc de Pompignan family, and Anne-Olympe had been brought up in friendship with the older son, Jean-Jacques. The following account of her family history, and in particular of her paternity, is only recorded in a novel Gouges advertised as autobiographical: *Memoires de Madame de Valmont* (1788). This epistolary novel is said by its author to give a true account of her mother's youth and of her own relations with her father's family. Because there are no official records of these events, we must confine ourselves to Gouges's accounts of herself in her writings. Fortunately, these are omnipresent in all her writings: *The Rights of Woman* gives a description of her proofreading habits, in the Preface to a 1788 play entitled *Le Philosophe Corrigé ou le Cocu Supposé* she describes her beauty routine.[2] What follows is a reconstruction based on Gouges's autobiographical writings.

Anne-Olympe and Jean-Jacques grew up together, and when they eventually fell in love, Jean-Jacques was sent away by his family who wished to avoid a marriage with a respectable but non-aristocratic family. After Jean-Jacques's departure, Anne-Olympe was married off to a butcher, Pierre Gouze, and over the next ten years, she gave birth to two daughters. In 1747 Jean-Jacques returned to Montauban and Gouze was sent to travel on business for a whole year. Anne-Olympe's third daughter, Marie (Olympe de Gouges), was born shortly after Gouze came back. There is no proof that Le Franc de Pompignan was Marie's father, but there is evidence that it was common knowledge in Montauban (Blanc, 2014: 21, note 14). When she came to Paris, Gouges tells us that she relied on rumours about her paternity to make her way into Parisian high society (Gouges, 1788a: 28).

---

[1] I used Olivier Blanc's 2014 biography *Olympe de Gouges* as well as Gouges's autobiographical works to write this biographical section. For more biography, see also Mousset (2007) and Scott (1997).

[2] https://fr.wikisource.org/wiki/Le_Philosophe_corrigé

Gouges was educated in a day school. The Ursulines school at Montauban had been started in 1682 by six Ursuline sisters from Toulouse. The school offered free classes to local girls in basic reading and writing, religious education, and sewing. The point of such an education was to prepare girls to become good Catholic wives. Thus Gouges's education was very limited, closer to what one might expect for the daughter of a butcher than for the grand-daughter of a lawyer or the daughter of an aristocrat. In the autobiographical novel *Memoires de Madame de Valmont*, Gouges (1788a) relates that her birth father had offered to take over her education but that her mother had, for some reason, refused. If we believe her autobiographical fiction to be an accurate reflection of her feelings, Gouges seemed not to bear a grudge. On the contrary, she enjoyed describing herself, as she did in her 'Preface pour les Dames', as a natural genius, who owed all her wisdom to Nature herself:

> Perhaps one day I will receive, without any effort on my part, the respect that is granted to works arisen from the hands of Nature. I can call myself one of its rare creations – everything I have comes from her; I have had no other tutor: and all my philosophical reflections cannot undo the strongly rooted imperfections that came with such an education (Gouges, 1788a: 7).

Nonetheless, as a result of an education that she regarded as neglected ('I had an education such as would have offered in the times of the great Bayard, and chance deprived me of light, in this most enlightened century' (Gouges, 1786: Preface)), she did have trouble working with pen and ink and was forced to hire secretaries to take down dictation for all her works. This was undoubtedly instrumental in her acquiring a reputation for illiteracy and the accusation of not being the author of her works. She attempted to respond to this slander through public dictation, but perverse rumour-mongers argued that she had been made to learn by heart the texts she dictated (Gouges, 1792a).

In 1765, when she was still a teenager, Marie Gouze was married to Louis-Yves Aubry, intendant in charge of food for the Count Alexis de Gourgues. In *Madame de Valmont* (Gouges, 1788a), she writes that her autobiographical heroine was married against her will and found her husband to be rude, unpleasant, and below her. She also noted that her mother inexplicably rejected another party she much preferred.

This marriage was in any case short-lived. Louis-Yves died in November 1766, three months after the birth of their son, Pierre Aubry (1766–1803). Although there is no record of his death, it is likely that he either drowned in the river Tarn, which inundated Montauban that year, or died after contracting one of the many diseases caused by the inundation.

The young widow, refusing to use her husband's name, became Olympe (later Marie-Olympe) de Gouges. Olympe was her mother's name, given her by her godmother, Anne-Olympe Colomb de la Pomarède. Gouges was a possible spelling of Gouze (Occitan was a spoken language more than a written one, so many words had alternative spellings), and 'de' a common way of saying 'daughter of'. Several political tracts of 1792 are signed 'Marie-Olympe de Gouges'. For legal papers, she signed 'Marie Gouze, Veuve Aubry'. In other texts, she refers to herself as 'Olympe de Gouges'. On one handwritten piece, she signs the postscript to a dictated letter in her own hand 'olimpe de gouges'.

A year after her husband's death, Gouges met Jacques Biétrix de Rozières, a military man who became her lover and helped finance her career. Although they remained close till her death, it would appear that she refused to marry him, preferring to stay single. It is possible that she already believed then what she later wrote in her *Declaration of the Rights of Woman*, that marriage was 'the tomb of trust and love' (Gouges, 1791). Rozières settled money and property on her, to an amount similar to what a marriage contract would have brought her (Blanc, 2014: 41).

Around 1769, Olympe gave birth to a daughter, Julie (at least that is how she is named in the autobiographical play *Bienfaisante ou la Bonne Mère* of 1788) (see Blanc, 2014: 40), who died in early childhood or infancy. The only (non-fictional) record of the baby girl's existence is in a statement Gouges made at her trial, when she claimed that she knew she was pregnant as she could recognize the symptoms that she was expecting from her first two pregnancies.

Gouges moved to Paris shortly after meeting Biétrix. There, according to her autobiographical novel, she met her half-brother, Pompignan's legitimate son, and their strong resemblance struck Parisian society so that she was welcomed into the homes of aristocrats. Gouges divided her time between her son, whose education she took very seriously, and mingling with Parisian artists and aristocrats. She became close friends with famous writer Louis-Sebastien Mercier (1740–1814) and future revolutionary politician Michel de Cubière (1752–1820). They introduced her to Madame de Montesson (1738–1806), who ran a private theatre in her Paris home. Montesson's stage manager was Joseph Bologne, Chevalier Saint Georges (1745–99), a 'man of colour', the son of a white planter and an enslaved woman from his plantation. Saint Georges was a composer who had been offered the management of the Paris Opera but had seen the offer withdrawn after some actresses had claimed they would not work with a Black manager. Saint Georges was also a military man, and had led the Revolutionary all-Black regiment. He was invested in the abolitionist move-ment and travelled to London, where he met the British Abolitionists, and later moved to Haiti to observe the Revolution's aftermath. It is possible that he served as a source of inspiration and information for Gouges's writings on slavery.

Acting with Madame de Montesson gave Gouges the opportunity to educate herself and refine her French accent and vocabulary. She did not start writing plays until 1784, and by then she had started her own amateur troupe in which she acted with her son, Pierre. Touring with her company proved invaluable for disseminating her work in France as she could not get her plays performed officially in the Paris theatres. Gouges had run afoul of theatrical politics, alienating all-powerful actors such as Fleury (1750–1822), who had the final say as to whether a play would be bought and performed. Only one of her plays, *Zamore and Mirza*, was ever performed in Paris, five years after it was submitted, and only for three nights. As well as performing them with her own company, Gouges ensured that her plays were known by publishing them at her own expense.

On the eve of the Revolution, Gouges went from being a political and philosophical playwright to defending her ideals more directly through pamphlet writing. Having witnessed the abject misery of the starving Parisians in the winter of 1788, she wrote her first political tract, asking the people of France to start a voluntary tax fund to ease the national debt and to feed the people. Her proposal, 'Lettre au people ou projet d'une caisse patriotique' (Gouges, 1788b), was printed on the front page of a national newspaper and, a few months later, eleven French women from an artistic milieu, led by the artist Adélaide-Marie-Castellas Moitte, donated jewels to the National Assembly. Two collection points were set up shortly afterwards. The first was set up by Madame Pajou, a daughter of a sculptor, who joined efforts with Madame Moitte to collect more jewels in the aftermath of the first donation. The second was the initiative of Madame Rigal, a goldsmith, who pronounced a discourse to a gathering of women artists and goldsmiths asking all women of France to follow the example of the eleven women from Versailles and help relieve the national debt.[3]

Gouges's political writing activity increased, and during the Revolution there were many placards by her, sometimes anonymous, sometimes signed, pasted around Paris. Her writings were often critical of the decisions of particular individuals in the government, including Robespierre. Her last tract, *The Three Urns* (1793c), advocating that the Paris Commune relinquish some of their power and put their motions to the vote through the whole of France, caused her to be arrested in July 1793 and guillotined in November of that year. Her final

---

[3] It may have been the case that several groups simultaneously decided to help relieve the national debt, but Gouges seemed persuaded that these particular groups acted because of her proposal, as witness another pamphlet written a few weeks later entitled 'My Wishes Are Fulfilled, or The Patriotic Gift. Dedicated to the Estates-General'.

months, described in the concluding section of this Element, displayed the same commitment to improving the social political situation of France as her earlier writings did. She died convinced that her memory would be avenged.

1.2 Playwright, Novelist, and Pamphleteer: Genre and Philosophy

Gouges's biographer, Olivier Blanc, lists 144 pieces of writing by her, including forty-three plays, sixty-eight tracts, placards, or articles, and thirty-one novels, prefaces, or isolated pieces.[4] All were written between 1784 and 1793. At least one of those pieces, *Primitive Happiness* (1789), can be described as a traditional piece of philosophical writing. It responds to J.-J. Rousseau's first two discourses, *On Science and the Arts* and *On Inequality*, and it develops the author's own account of the origins of human society and of their ethical and political implications. But much of what Gouges wrote – be it plays, novels, or articles and open letters published in papers and as placards – was philosophical. The author used formats she was comfortable with – often formats that used a spoken style of rhetoric, such as theatre or speech-making – and at the same time, formats she knew would reach a wider audience than would an academic article – a text written by a member of an academy, destined for the local intelligentsia.

Unlike the tracts of her contemporaries, who often sought to denounce or publicize a particular political stance, decision, or personality, Gouges's writings stand out for their use of argumentation and her clear desire to make her readers think and come to their own conclusions rather than simply accept hers. The pamphlet she was arrested and convicted for, *The Three Urns* (Gouges, 1793c), is a case in point: Gouges asked that the people of France be allowed to consider what form of government would best protect their rights, rather than have that decision imposed on them by Robespierre and Danton. In a similar vein, her writings on slavery (a play, a preface, a pamphlet, and an open letter), although they clearly denounce the practice of enslaving human beings, also offer reflections on why that practice is wrong and what courses of action might be morally justified for those who find themselves enslaved and those who want to help free them.

As I hope to demonstrate in what follows, Gouges's reflections on women's situation in society, the rights they are entitled to, the role they might play in obtaining rights for themselves and others, and how the might help society flourish are present in her novels, her plays, and her pamphlets and longer texts,

---

[4] For a full list, see Blanc, 2014: 238–47. There are very few recent editions or translations of Gouges's works, but most of them can be found in French on Gallica, the website of the BNF (https://bit.ly/37JXGtE), and many have been translated by Clarissa Palmer and posted on her webpage (www.olympedegouges.eu).

such as *Primitive Happiness* (1789). The most famous of these texts is evidently her *Declaration of the Rights of Woman* (1791). Gouges contemplates through these texts the place of women in humanity and the nature of humanity itself. Her argument for equality comes from an understanding of what it means to be human. But unlike her contemporary, Mary Wollstonecraft, she does not focus on the capacity to reason. Human beings, for Gouges, are first and foremost creatures who are capable of living and working together, who can learn while they emulate, and who depend on each other for growth and support throughout their lives. Given the importance of community for human flourishing, it makes sense that women should be seen as equally important to men: communities can only grow through families. Her stance on marriage is closely related to her political philosophy. Gouges is a republican (despite her early attempts at defending the king) who believes that a sound political system which enables the flourishing of citizens should be free of domination, whether that domination comes from hereditary tyrannical power or newly imposed dictatorships. Marriage also, she argues, needs to be free of domination, as a union without freedom will not enable the growth of virtue, and hence happiness.

Even though Gouges's literary and theatrical pieces have a political and ethical message which they develop through philosophical argument, we should also consider her views on what role aesthetics can play in society. Although she partially agrees with Rousseau that too much art is a sign of social decadence, she also believes that he was wrong to see theatre as doing nothing more than pandering to a perverse audience, and acting as a way of infiltrating society with women who ought to be tucked away in their homes.

1.3 A Note on Gender

Olympe de Gouges argued for women to be granted the same civil rights as men. But there are many parts of her work that seem to suggest that she would have been in favour of a difference feminism, one which took into consideration the specificity of female virtues, and argued that they had a role to play in the shaping of the republic. Women could be female and active citizens; they had something specific to bring to politics. This is a view developed by Martina Reuter (2019: 407), following Smart (2011), who argued that Gouges appealed to women's expertise as mothers to argue that home life was also a form of civic life. This was a belief held also by Gouges's friend, the playwright Sébastien Mercier, who, in his futuristic novel *L'An 2440* (1771), appeals to motherhood in order to rethink the body politic (Smart, 2011: 75).

Gouges frequently appeals to women's experience, as mothers and wives, and the way in which this experience affects their virtue. The institution of marriage, she says, makes women dishonest and conniving (Gouges, 1791), and their status as daughters means they are uneducated and unable to fend for themselves if they are widowed (Gouges, 2014). But these characteristics are tied to women's circumstances, not their essence. Appeals to virtues that are related to motherhood could be either. One could argue that women, through the experience of mothering, develop certain character traits and virtues or that women have certain natural virtues that they are called on to exercise when they become mothers. It is not clear that Gouges believes the latter, rather than the former. Some of her reflections on gender – her own and that of others – suggest, on the contrary, that she found it to be fluid.

In *Départ de Necker, ou les adieux de Madame de Gouges aux Français et A M. Necker*, Gouges describes herself as 'A woman who long ago made herself a man in order to be able to say what she wanted to say' (Gouges, 1790a). This has been read as evidence that she thought women had to acquire men's characteristics in order to participate in politics, or at least that she herself 'emulated and appropriated' the role of the active citizen in order to claim citizenship for women (Scott, 1997: 56). Later in the same text, Gouges says that she had to overcome her 'feminine timidity' in order to address the king and queen and advise them to call back Necker (Gouges, 1790a). But neither of these suggest that she had to overcome her nature. In fact, the ease with which she apparently switches between masculine and feminine personas suggests, on the contrary, that these are superficial traits, masks she can put on and off. This is not to say that all gendered traits are superficial and easy to discard or adopt: some are the product of lifelong habit, and prejudice, and have become second nature. But second nature is not essential nature, and this, I think, is what distinguishes Gouges's views on gender from difference feminism.

Other writings also support the idea that Gouges's views of gender characteristics were fluid and that gender was acquired rather than essential. This is true, in particular, of her references to Madame d'Eon. Madame d'Eon, previously Chevalier d'Eon, was a well-known diplomat who identified as a woman from her midlife until her death, and moved to London to make a living as a celebrity swordfighter. Although some Londoners seemed to be unsure about d'Eon's gender of origin at her death, it is unlikely that Gouges did not know that d'Eon had lived half her life as a man. Madame d'Eon only became known as a woman in 1777, by which time Gouges was a part of Parisian society and would have noted the transitioning of a famous chevalier, yet she refers to herself as belonging to the same 'sex':

> Mademoiselle Déon [sic] proves only too well that my sex is not lacking in courage. I will admit there are few with this martial character, but there have

been some. And you who are more fearful than women, do you not fear this sex that has distinguished itself in other circumstances, and may I, myself, convince you that Mademoiselle Déon has transmitted to me her intrepidity?

(Gouges, 1789: 112)[5]

Given that she uses a trans woman as a model for herself, it is unlikely that she would have had a view of feminine virtues as tied to a biological woman's essence. Also, as many other writings suggest that she thinks typical feminine traits are acquired through circumstances (the fact that girls do not receive sufficient education, that women are dominated in marriage), it would seem that Gouges is not, on the whole, inclined to argue for a form of difference feminism.

1.4 Overview of Recent Scholarship and Note on the Texts

Works on Olympe de Gouges as a philosopher are few and far between. Nevertheless, others have written about her, and it is fitting to give an overview of recent scholarship here. Three recent monographs are dedicated to Gouges's work: John Cole's 2011 *Between the Queen and the Cabby*, Carol Sherman's 2013 *Reading Olympe de Gouges*, and Olivier Blanc's 2014 *Olympe de Gouges*. Cole's book offers a translation and a commentary on Gouges's *Rights of Woman*. Unfortunately, Cole announces in the introduction that Gouges was 'no philosopher' (5), which makes it difficult to look for help understanding Gouges's philosophy in his book. Sherman presents Gouges as a dramaturge who used theatrical rhetoric in all her works. She also emphasizes the extent to which calumnious gossip about Gouges has prevented her from becoming the influential philosopher she ought to be. I take up this important theme in my final section, when I discuss her reputation. Blanc's book-length biography (in French) is an exemplary resource for details of Gouges's life and for the context necessary to understand her various publications. Gouges wrote a large number of political pamphlets, the significance of which was in part determined by the events they responded to. Blanc's carefully referenced work makes this reconstruction easier.

Others have, in the past thirty years or so, discussed Gouges's contribution to philosophy and feminism in chapter-length works. Erica Harth in *Cartesian Women* (1992) discusses Gouges's relationship with Condorcet's and Rousseau's writings, showing that while she is close to both, she also disagrees with them. Joan Scott, in her *Only Paradoxes to Offer* (1997), discusses Gouges as a feminist writer and concentrates on her various arguments for giving women rights of citizenship. Scott reads Gouges's efforts to combat revolutionary sexism as an attempt to infuse the masculine concept of citizenship with a feminine

---

[5] Interestingly, in her *Vindication of the Rights of Woman*, published in 1792, Wollstonecraft also listed Madame d'Eon as an exemplary woman.

imagination. Blanc (2014) criticized Scott for imposing an anachronistic distinction between equality feminism and difference feminism back onto Gouges and her contemporaries. Mary Seidman Trouille, in her *Sexual Politics in the Enlightenment* (1997), writes about Gouges as a reader of Rousseau, focussing on Gouges's reaction to Rousseau's views on women in his *Emile* and *Letter to D'Alembert*. Annie Smart, in *Citoyennes* (2011), has a chapter on Gouges in which she discusses several of her writings up to and including the *Rights of Woman*, focussing her interpretation on the female embodiment of Gouges's arguments. She argues that Gouges ultimately understands women's civic participation to be home-bound. Karen Green, in *A History of Women's Political Thought in Europe, 1700–1800* (2014), discusses the apparent contradiction between Gouges's feminism and her political views – according to Green, monarchism. In this Element, I refer to these works but ultimately propose a different account of Gouges, as a feminist political philosopher who was a republican in the neo-Roman sense, dedicated to inclusive equality and to human progress, a progress fuelled by collaboration and emulation.

There are very few recent editions or translations of Gouges's works, but most of them can be found in French on Gallica, the website of the BNF,[6] and many have been translated by Clarissa Palmer and posted on her webpage.[7] I have chosen, whenever possible, to refer to texts that are easily available online. Where I give quotes from texts that have no translation listed in the bibligraphy, the translation is mine.

1.5 Outline

In the three following sections I will give an overview of some of Gouges's arguments, showing their originality and their relevance to debates contemporary to her and to us. In Section 1, I will begin with a discussion of her views on education, human progress, and social reform, which Gouges presents in a 1789 short treatise, *Primitive Happiness*. This provides an opportunity to situate Gouges's philosophy in relation to that of her contemporaries, in particular Rousseau, but also Gouges's views on human nature and the ways in which it could grow are central to her political philosophy. Shortly after *Primitive Happiness* was published, Gouges's work became closely intertwined with the historical events of the French Revolution. Accordingly, in Sections 3 and 4, I will present her views on liberty and on equality. In the final section I will draw out Gouges's lasting influence and the relevance of her work for contemporary philosophers.

---

[6] https://bit.ly/37M4LtF.   [7] www.olympedegouges.eu.

2 Education, Progress, and Social Reform

The possibility of human progress was an important concern for eighteenth-century philosophers.[8] The efforts of Enlightenment philosophers to cast aside superstition and replace it with science, the push towards social reform, and the promise inherent in the three major revolutions – first in America, then France, and then Haiti – all pointed to the possibility of change for the better. This optimism was particularly salient in the case of those who had been most oppressed, such as women and those who had been enslaved. Men who had escaped slavery wrote about it and toured Europe to convince others that the practices of enslaving human beings and trading them ought to stop. They met political reformers in France and England and jointly worked towards abolition. Some women philosophers too saw in the new reforms the opportunity for the inclusion of their sex, and they used their platforms as writers to attempt to hasten that progress. In England, Mary Wollstonecraft dedicated her *Vindication of the Rights of Woman* to the Marquis de Talleyrand, whom the French government had asked to prepare a proposal for reforming national education. In France, Olympe de Gouges, who was already a well-known pamphleteer at that time, responded to the Declaration of the Rights of Man and of the Citizen by publishing her own *Declaration of the Rights of Woman*. The consensus at the time seemed to be that, if progress was happening, everyone ought to benefit from it.

Not every eighteenth-century philosopher was sanguine about the possibility of progress: Rousseau had famously argued in his *Discourse on the Arts and Sciences* that social innovations prevented, rather than facilitated, human progress. Edmund Burke had argued that social reforms such as the ones advanced in revolutionary France would destroy the fragile framework that made human interactions tolerable by hiding the worst of our natures behind social niceties, 'the decent drapery of life' (Burke, 1986: 171).

Gouges's intervention in that debate goes against both Rousseau and Burke. She believed that human nature is such that we can work together towards social progress and that education and the arts, properly understood, will help progress along. Although her faith in human progress is visible in many of her writings, particularly the *Rights of Woman* (Gouges, 1791) but also her several proposals for very practical reforms – for a voluntary tax (Gouges, 1788b) and for building a hospice for women (Gouges, 2014) – her arguments are most clearly and extensively set out in her more traditionally philosophical book: *Primitive Happiness* (Gouges, 1789).

---

[8] Some of the argument of this section is drawn from Bergès (2018).

The text is divided into five numbered chapters followed by three unnumbered ones. It offers a speculative account of primitive human societies that suggests that Rousseau and Hobbes were wrong to think that primitive human societies could not function without a state, and presents Gouges's argument that the root to human social happiness is a particular form of education, through 'emulation', which can be achieved through common work and the arts. The first five chapters engage with Rousseau's first two discourses: the *Discourse on the Arts and Sciences* (1997) and the *Discourse on the Origins of Inequality* (1997). The first of the unnumbered chapters, 'The Project for a Second French Theatre', can be read as a conclusion for the argument of the treatise as a whole. The two chapters that follow the 'Project' are perhaps best read as an afterword.

Rousseau's first two discourses describe primitive societies and the effect of civilization on the progress (or regress) of humankind. Gouges's book attempts to answer two questions: were primitive human societies happy, and, if so, how was that happiness lost? Like Rousseau in his first *Discourse*, Gouges displays a certain amount of scepticism as to whether education, culture, science, and the arts in general may contribute to human happiness. But Gouges doesn't reject culture, science, or education, except those forms of education that are expected to contribute not to the happiness or well-being of the student but to their social advancement.

> Learned men and lovers of the sciences feel sorry, they say, for these ignorant men who feared no danger, and who were ignorant of humanity itself. One should therefore suppose that nature had refused them everything, and drove them to the centuries of voracious ambition and unimpeded depravation in order to teach them how to be happy and enlightened. Ah! I must beg to differ and presume that man has too far extended his knowledge. He is now at the last period and by seeking too much, he has moved away from the truth, and only finds the kind of ignorance that tires his judgment and, in the end, misleads his reason. (Gouges, 1789: 19–20)

And again:

> I do not disdain the sciences, although my bizarre star wished me to be ignorant; it is the abuse I condemn. What man is not a savant at the present time? (Gouges, 1789: 22)

Gouges agrees with Rousseau that excessive indulgence in the arts leads to unhappiness, when that indulgence is paid for by the misery of others:

> The arts, I know, enrich a kingdom; but when they are pushed to the last degree, they indubitably bring with them luxury, and luxury, sluggishness; thus luxury destroys all Nations. I appeal to those wise men to whom I submit these Dreams. (Gouges, 1789: 57–8)

But Gouges also believes that the arts are a fundamental part of human development and happiness, and that when properly integrated in social institutions, they will also benefit politics. In the chapter entitled 'Project for a Second Theatre', she argues that primitive happiness can be regained if social institutions take control of the arts by setting up a state theatre that privileges artistic expression over the entertainment of the rich and offers training and patronage for genuine artists – writers or actors – focussing on talent instead of popularity.

One strong link between the discussion of primitive societies at the beginning and social reform through the arts at the end is the principle of emulation, a form of progress through competition and imitation. The nature of that concept was much disputed in the late eighteenth and early nineteenth centuries, with some, such as Rousseau's disciple, Bernardin de Sain-Pierre, arguing that it destroyed moral character by making children aggressively competitive, while others, such as Gouges and Madame de Stael, believed it was a natural way for human beings to develop and learn to work together. This section will show how Gouges believed human progress was possible through emulation.

2.1 Poverty and Decadence

Much of the early modern and Enlightenment discourse on human progress started from a description of primitive human societies. The point was either to understand where we had started from or to posit a hypothesis, in an attempt to isolate what was at the core of human essence or what we would have started from had we been suddenly thrown into a naked environment, with items added, progressively, so that changes may be observed.

An equally important touchstone for a study of human progress was the present, the conditions of life in the contemporary world. Are human beings better, or happier, now than they would have been in primitive societies? What are the structures that make or prevent their happiness? Often, it was present conditions that led philosophers to reflect on what had gone wrong and what could go better. So Hobbes thought of the civil war when he wrote that, without strong authority to govern them, human beings would revert to a state of nature that was a state of constant war of all against all. Similarly, Rousseau wanted to look away from the decadence of the luxury-loving French aristocrats when he described the simple lives of primitive human beings, tracing the moment when all had started to go wrong to the discovery that they could compete with each other through the arts. The arts, especially the theatre, then, was the scourge of human society and to be avoided at all costs for those societies that still had a chance of being saved, such as Geneva – Paris, Rousseau thought, was already lost.

Gouges's programme is similar to Rousseau's: 'I will examine, without discrimination, all that characterizes the stupidity of mankind since its loss of happiness. I will observe it in all its pleasures, ambition, torments, hypocrisy, villainy and hopes' (Gouges, 1789: 2). And like him, she intends to assess human progress: 'Therefore, I will take man as he comes out of the hands of nature, follow him up to the point to which he has arrived, and offer a glimpse of the state he could fall back to' (Gouges, 1789: 6–7).

But here, the most obvious similarities between Gouges's and Rousseau's projects end. Olympe de Gouges traced the trouble of humanity as arising not from the progress of the arts but from poverty. Observing the effects on Parisians of the cold weather and the rising price of bread in the winter of 1788, she felt a 'deep despair' for workers who could not feed their children and turned to violence, and perhaps would go as far as civil war, to remedy their wants (Gouges, 1788b). Far from wanting to applaud this early revolutionary spirit – a year before the Revolution – Gouges was wary of anyone who might encourage it, as it would, she thought, push those who suffered now deeper into misery. This observation is the premise to her *Project for a Patriotic Fund* (Gouges, 1788b), which encouraged actresses and women artists to donate their excess wealth in order to reduce the national deficit. While Gouges did not entirely disagree with Rousseau that the arts were somehow to blame, as she saw men who were struggling to feed their families spend what little they had on entertainment, she did not see the arts as symptomatic in the same way. The main symptom for Gouges was poverty and the inability to provide for one's family.

Gouges made the same point in her *Projet utile et salutaire* (2014), where she observed that in difficult times workers live and die horribly. She suggested that we owe them any help we can give them without at the same time taking away from them the means of providing for their own needs, should more favourable conditions return. The *Projet utile* was written when some of the walls surrounding Paris were to be demolished, and a great deal of stone suddenly became available. Gouges proposed that this stone be used to build hospices for the people, and in particular one hospice for women who had fallen on hard times, where their physical and psychological health would be nurtured and some attempt would be made at redressing the many wrongs done to them simply because they are women and therefore not educated or given opportunities to flourish, or at least survive, in the world without the protection of men.

In *Primitive Happiness*, Gouges observes that there is a disconnect between the luxury in which the rich live and the abject poverty of those who work for them:

> It must also be recognized that the Lords, the wealthy, do not live enough in the countryside; that they do not share their benefits with their vassals. They have never sought to render the existence of the Peasants happy or peaceful. Yet it is the Labourers whose labouring hands have unearthed the treasures of the soil, and all the delights of the great and rich. What compassionate soul softens the rigour of their fate! What generous heart comes to succour them in their infirmity, which most often has been caused by their excessive efforts and travails! They feed men yet lack bread themselves. (Gouges, 1789: 52)

Whatever the state of nature might be for Gouges, it is clear from her observations of poverty that she thought civil society could be improved. Although the idea that the state of nature was a dangerous one and that any form of civil society would be better for human beings was popular among philosophers, it was not as appealing to Gouges.

2.2 Primitive Societies and Emulation

Many of those engaged in the debate on progress made some assumptions or posited hypotheses about primitive societies and about what life before civil society and what they regarded as civilization must have been like. In many cases, the picture that was drawn of humans in their primitive state was rather dark and unpleasant, carrying the message that, however much we might complain about living in governed societies, we are in fact much better off than we would be if we did not. This was most famously the case for Hobbes, who described the state of nature as a state of 'constant war of all against all' (Hobbes, 1986: 185). So bad was the state of nature for Hobbes that we ought to welcome any ruler capable of drawing us out, and especially keeping us out, of it. Though Rousseau is known as a gentler sort of political philosopher, his picture of the state of nature is in fact just as stark as Hobbes's. His primitive human beings were peaceful as long as they lived alone and as animals, but as soon as necessity brought them closer to each other, they grew competitive and 'bloodthirsty and cruel' (Rousseau, 1997: 166).

Gouges disagreed with Rousseau, and although she did not engage directly with Hobbes, it is clear she would also have disagreed with him. Primitive humans, she thought, had always lived in societies, and their progress had only been possible because they were capable of working together, first to feed themselves and later to innovate. She was sympathetic to Rousseau's diagnosis of the degeneration of eighteenth-century society and his view that science and the arts were no longer a means to progress for anything except decadence. The arts and science entertained the rich and kept them from having to strive for anything, while they convinced the poor to give up on useful or healthy pursuits, sending them to the towns in search of social advancement and glory that could never be theirs (Gouges, 1789: 57, 52).

Gouges thought that in early societies human beings were happy. In order to regain this primitive happiness and move towards a better existence, she argued that human beings needed to go back to a collaborative and 'emulative' model of existence, which she saw as characteristic of primitive societies and a move away from the thirst for individual betterment through learning or 'instruction'.

One major difference between Gouges's and Rousseau's pictures of primitive societies, then, was that for Rousseau early human gatherings inevitably turned violent through competition, while for Gouges they were first and foremost peaceful and collaborative. What allows her to see human beings as naturally collaborative is her focus on the (extended) family unit, rather than the individual. Rousseau all but wrote women and families out of his accounts of primitive human existence, portraying primitive humans as always lonely and shying away from associating with others for more than brief encounters. These solitary beings are able to remain peaceful and happy as long as they do not form into societies, which in the first instance involves gathering into family units, at which point they become 'bloodthirsty and cruel' towards each other. These early creatures were also amoral, as Rousseau noted that in order to develop true compassion one needed to be exposed to another's suffering at length (Rousseau, 1997: 154), and this could not happen if all encounters were brief. Given his insistence on early humans' lone existence, Rousseau's account of how the human race persevered longer than one generation may strike us as rather implausible: in order to prevent family groups from developing, Rousseau's primitive babies must become independent very soon after birth. One senses that Rousseau gave less thought to his account of the lives of human females. A male human may of course have elected to keep his encounters with others brief but, even with babies gaining independence after a few years, females would inevitably have been around infants long enough to develop a sense of the suffering of others and some skill in reducing it. And if any one female had several children during her fertile years, it is to be expected that these children, male as well as female, would also have had the chance to learn compassion. So, by being blind to the fate of one half of humanity, as well as to the fact that human beings must be dependent on one another at least at the beginning of their lives, Rousseau offered a skewed picture of what early humans may have been like.

Women and family finally take up their place in human history in Rousseau's second *Discourse*, at the point when resources are no longer plentiful and the lone humans decide to gather in villages. They become sedentary and women are confined to the homes. But rather than bringing happiness, this common living brings about competition:

> As soon as men had begun to appreciate one another and the idea of
> consideration had taken shape in their mind, everyone claimed a right to it,
> and one could no longer deprive anyone of it with impunity.. ... Vengeances
> became terrible and men blood-thirsty and cruel. This is precisely the stage
> reached by most of the Savage Peoples known to us; and it is for want of
> drawing adequate distinctions between ideas and noticing how far these
> Peoples already were from the first state of nature that so many hastened to
> conclude that man is naturally cruel and needs political order in order to be
> made gentle, whereas nothing is as gentle as he in his primitive state.
>
> (Rousseau, 1997: 166)

Gouges, in *Primitive Happiness*, differs from Rousseau primarily in that she
does not believe that primitive human societies were unhappy or that their
natural goodness had already been corrupted. In the first two chapters of
Primitive Happiness, she paints a picture of human beings who are capable of
happiness and of a life that remains free from domination as long as it is a simple
life in which everyone seeks to be useful to others.

At the beginning of chapter one, she has a dying elder telling his descendants
what it is that makes them strong and how they should carry on:

> You must cultivate the earth, and as you make new discoveries, you will see
> emulation spread among you. Your goods should be held communally, your
> portions equal, your dress and housing the same, your manners simple and
> sweet; The eve of a harvest will be a holiday. Those who suffer will always
> find relief from those who are strong and healthy; children will serve fathers,
> younger brothers their elders, except in cases of sickness. . . . All will without
> distinction participate to the public good, without having the opportunity to
> refuse under any pretext expect infirmity or sickness. Women who breastfeed
> their children will be exempt from public works. (Gouges, 1789: 13–14)

Life in Gouges's primitive society is thus simple and healthy, and it encourages
trust and collaboration rather than distrust. Note, however, that this is not
because competition is absent: she talks of emulation. But, for her, competition
is a result not of conflict between individuals who want to outdo each other but
of a drive to better serve the community collectively. We'll come back to this in
the last part of this section.

There is a fine line, however, between the sort of emulation that leads to
progress that benefits the public good and that which drives a wedge between
those who are successful and those who are not, and ultimately results in the
domination of some by others. Gouges turns to this worry and the fragility of
happiness in chapter two of *Primitive Happiness*.

At the end of chapter one, Gouges explains that the crowning glory of the
society she describes is an act that unites people who are attracted to each other
and choose to be with each other, thus appealing to Nature and human

institutions at the same time. Couples swear an indissoluble tie to each other in a temple standing on top of a mountain. This act epitomizes both the union of human society to nature and the idea that this is a society of willing interdependence, rather than one of lone creatures forced to live together by need. But anyone familiar with Gouges's views on marriage and divorce, in particular that marriage is the tomb of love, will know that something dangerous is afoot. Gouges believed that a marriage that cannot be dissolved through divorce was tantamount to a set of chains that would prevent all but the most heroic husbands and wives from wanting to live virtuously. And indeed, at the beginning of chapter two, her primitive society is shaken to its core by an act of marital infidelity. A married man tires of his wife and falls in love with another woman. They are found out on the day of the first solar eclipse ever witnessed. This is interpreted as Nature's punishment and the cheating couple is cast off.

During their exile, the couple make many discoveries, which enrich themselves and their growing family. They also learn the mechanics of planetary movements, and they return to the village when the next eclipse is due, able to predict its beginning and its end. The villagers are first shocked and then impressed by what they see as a manipulation of the sun, and superstition makes them acclaim the newcomers as their leaders, a position that is reinforced by their superior technological abilities. Soon enough, a particularly ambitious subset of the village manipulate the older villagers' superstitions and institutionalize their beliefs into a monotheistic cult of the Sun. The self-styled priests of the Sun, who are willing to demean humanity for their own advancement, ensure that the primitive society becomes a dominated one.

The belief that it is institutionalized religion and the priestly class that are responsible for introducing systematic relations of domination in human societies is one shared by other contemporaries of Gouges, in particular Condorcet. Condorcet argued, in his posthumously published *Sketch for a Historical Picture of the Progress of the Human Mind*, that the advent of institutionalized religion and the creation of a class of priests were to blame for much of the difficulties and failures of humanity (Condorcet, 2012: 26). While Gouges did not read the *Sketch*, which was unwritten at the time of her death, she may well have been familiar with Condorcet's views, and these views would have been shared by many members of the Girondin faction (of which she and Condorcet were members, as were Brissot and Marie-Jeanne and Jean Marie Roland). It was in fact the atheism of his Girondist friends that led Thomas Paine to pen his *Age of Reason*, hoping to persuade them to take a more (to his mind) reasonable and deist position (Bergès, 2019b: 63–4).

Although Gouges's argument resembles Condorcet's at the beginning, the direction it takes is rather different. Condorcet argues that priests stifle human progress by preventing the dissemination of knowledge. In *Primitive Happiness*, things happen somewhat differently. The domination of the priests leads to the creation of a class of servants to work for them. The servants are brought up in a state of ignorance and eventually forget what their ancestors knew: that all human beings were originally equal. Eventually, those servants too become touched by ambition and seek social elevation through any means, including education. But by that time, Gouges explains, education has become no more than an aid to ambition and cannot help them regain the essential knowledge they lost when they were first subdued by the priests.

In chapter three, Gouges continues to argue that education, when it is ill-conceived, endangers the happiness of societies. Primitive happiness, she argues, is fragile, and it is vulnerable to so-called progress in the sciences and the arts and to a certain sort of education, that is, 'learning' or the passing on of information without any goal other than that of filling the heads of students and giving them (false) grounds for thinking themselves superior to others (Gouges uses the French '*instruction*', which suggests learning by rote without reflection). This kind of education, she says, brings about luxury and weakness of the kind that caused the fall of ancient civilizations (Gouges, 1789: 57). Here, Gouges is in agreement with Rousseau's views in *Emile* (Rousseau, 1979: 107) and Wollstonecraft's in the *Vindication of the Rights of Woman* (Wollstonecraft, 2014: 144): that education should not take the form of learning information by heart. Such activity, Gouges, Rousseau, and Wollstonecraft concur, cannot extend the mind's capacity for grasping the world and can only produce such superficial learning as may be ridiculed by others. For Wollstonecraft, it also reinforces the social inferiority of women, for it is they who are mocked for not having any deep knowledge but only being able to repeat what others have told them (Wollstonecraft, 2014: 144). This, incidentally, is what Gouges reported as having happened to her: a man – who did not know who she was – informed her that the famous Olympe de Gouges was an illiterate who could only repeat texts that had been written for her and that she had been taught what to say (Gouges, 1792a).

For Wollstonecraft, the only remedy to gender inequality is to afford women the same education as men and to stop using rote learning altogether as an educational method for children. Gouges's objection to rote learning also has a social dimension. Such learning, she says, undermines the division of labour necessary for the well-being of society and the expertise that goes with specialization, while at the same time creating a false sense of equality. The poor may fancy themselves equal to the rich when they have received a similar education, but the rich know to keep their advantage: 'We want to be equal, but with superiority, will say the richest, and the reformers of laws' (Gouges, 1789: 64).

When social inequality is marked by great shows of wealth on the one side and great poverty on the other, Gouges remarks, it is natural that the very poor should envy the lifestyle of the very rich. Thus it comes about that the ambition of the poor is not to divest themselves of poverty and simply to better their lives but to imitate the rich. This, however, they cannot truly do – learning to ape the rich by going to their schools and learning their way of life does not result in being offered a place in high society or the means to retain that place. Gouges, who moved from an artisan household in the south of France into Parisian aristocratic circles, knows that well. Had she not successfully crafted for herself a career as a writer, she may well have become what some historians claim she was: a high-class prostitute.

So if learning by rote is not the key to human progress, what is Gouges's recommendation in *Primitive Happiness*? She does not claim that we should go back to a primitive lifestyle, abandoning any cultural or scientific progress we may have made. But she asks that we do not blindly trust in the ability of such progress to see to our natural needs. The lesson Gouges wishes to draw from her reflections is that rather than instruction, which for Gouges is a solitary pursuit to improve oneself by ingesting other people's formulas, it is emulation – a collaborative type of learning – that enriches human life and culture. This will be elaborated in the following subsection.

2.3 Emulation and Progress through the Arts

Nowhere does Gouges give a full and direct account of what she would regard as proper schooling, that is, the right sort of education to be dispensed to young people. This is perhaps because she does not believe that 'schooling' is a positive part of educating children, or that it can be separated from the habit of 'instructing' or forcing children to learn by rote. But what she does talk about rather a lot, in *Primitive Happiness* in particular, is the role of the arts in education. In order to present the clearest possible picture of what Gouges has to say about education through the arts, I will begin by showing how Gouges rejects Rousseau's conception of the arts as generally harmful to society, focussing on their disagreement about the meaning and function of 'emulation'. Next, I will show how Gouges conceived of a scheme to reform the French theatre that would also serve a number of educational purposes: educating the public through improving plays, educating children whose future is uncertain by creating a school for them, and educating actors to perform in such a way that society will benefit from their performance.

Gouges's disagreement with Rousseau centres around the concept of emulation, a complex concept that, in the first instance, we will understand to mean competition. Like Hobbes before him, Rousseau blamed what he perceived as the violence inherent in early human societies on the drive to compete. But Hobbes believed that competition and the character traits that derive from it were the product of the fact that human beings are roughly equal in bodily strength and intellect, alongside a scarcity of resources in the state of nature. Human beings discovered that, in order to feed themselves, they sometimes needed to fight others who had an equal claim to the goods they wanted, and an equal ability to get to them. For Hobbes, this led not only to a desire to fight to survive in the face of scarcity ('competition') but also to a desire to be recognized by others as superior ('glory') so as to counteract a fear of what others may do to us or take from us ('diffidence') – which, in turn, aids 'competition'. Hobbes made sure to add that he was not thereby condemning human nature, as until a society under the rule of law exists, people have little to drive them in this 'state of war' but their own desire for survival and safety (Hobbes, 1986: 186).

Whereas, for Hobbes, competition was at least in part the result of a scarcity of resources and does not imply a condemnation of human nature, Rousseau thought competition was the direct result of human beings coming into contact with each other. Unlike Hobbes, who claimed that humans in the state of nature are equal, Rousseau saw them as fundamentally unequal in terms of the qualities that they desired: being good-looking or a good singer or dancer, for example. Human beings who saw others as possessing these qualities more so than they were jealous to the point of wanting to annihilate the competition, and displays of talent in the performing arts were ways of signalling one's superiority:

> Singing and dancing, the true offspring of love and leisure, became the amusement, or rather the occupation, of men and women thus assembled together with nothing else to do. Each one began to consider the rest, and to wish to be considered in turn; and thus a value came to be attached to public esteem. Whoever sang or danced best, whoever was the handsomest, the strongest, the most dexterous, or the most eloquent, came to be of most consideration; and this was the first step towards inequality, and at the same time towards vice. (Rousseau, 1997: 166)

Anyone reading this will be struck by the sudden move from dancing as an amusement to dancing as the means to gather admiration. Rousseau does not seem to consider that enjoyment of the arts, whether as spectator or performer, may have intrinsic value or contribute to human happiness. Dancing and singing may be natural pursuits, but, according to Rousseau, they inevitably lead to ambition and ranking. In Gouges's primitive society, those pursuits are part of life long before the first step towards decadence appears. The people she depicts in chapter one of *Primitive Happiness* are seen to enjoy themselves in their sweet and simple ways, and it is only the too severe restrictions imposed by their marriage vows, and not enjoyment or pleasure, that lead to unpleasantness.

Rousseau was clearly attached to his view of the performing arts as conducive to harmful competition, as three years after writing the *Discourse on Inequality*, where he explained how dancing and singing led to competition, he argued, in his *Letter to D'Alembert*, that theatre had the same effect on contemporary societies (Rousseau, 1968). *Letter* is a response to D'Alembert's 1757 *Encyclopedia* entry on the Republic of Geneva, in which he argues that it would be improved if it were to have a national theatre. Rousseau replies that such an institution would in fact bring down the republic. The performing arts, he says, only exacerbate the natural human drive to competition, and will revive any vanity that the republican virtue of the Genevans kept at bay. Ultimately, this will make them unfit for self-government. One major source of theatrical corruption, Rousseau thinks, is the actors, and in particular actresses. He sees these as prostitutes who advertise their wares onstage to an already paying, and at first unsuspecting, public. The theatre thus encourages depravity, chipping at civic virtue under the guise of art and education, until eventually there is none left.

Gouges's take on the role of competition, in particular competition through the arts, is quite the opposite to Rousseau's. As far as she is concerned, competition is beneficial to the strengthening of human societies, leading to better collaboration and hence progress, and the performance arts are a healthy way of practising competition. In her writings, Gouges refers to 'emulation' rather than 'competition'. However, it is clear that she is referring to that which Rousseau condemns. Jacques-Henri Bernardin de Saint-Pierre, a disciple of Rousseau who believed in the ultimate goodness of human nature, thought that emulation was always harmful because it was in fact a sort of a competition that engendered jealousy and all sorts of other social ills. In a text on reforming national education, he explained why emulation ought to be avoided in education:

> They will therefore banish emulation from their schools . . . Emulation is the cause of most of the ills of the human race. . . . It is the root of ambition, for emulation generates the desire to be first . . . [It] generates . . . theft, prostitution, charlatanism, superstition . . . jealousy, slander, calomnies, quarrels, trials, duels, intolerance . . . taxes, slavery, tyrannies and war. . . . For a long time I believed that ambition was natural to man; but today I regard it as simply a result of our education (Saint-Pierre, 1836: 171).

The word 'émulation' in eighteenth-century French was ambiguous, and its meaning was contested. At its most neutral, it referred to the desire to do as well as or better than others but without necessarily a desire to outdo the other. Emulation in that sense meant competition but not rivalry. But it was also taken to refer to the sort of competition which entailed, as Bernardin de Saint-Pierre noted, coming first, rather than simply being as good as one can be. That there were two possible meanings was no secret: the Abbé Roubaud, in his popular 1786 *Dictionary of Synonyms*, had distinguished them clearly (85–9). So it was a matter of philosophical interpretation of the concept that led some to think of emulation as harmful and others not, rather than a simple lexical disagreement.

Gouges uses the word 'emulation' fourteen times in her 125-page treatise. She first introduces it in the speech of the dying elder telling his family how to grow:

> You must cultivate the earth, and as you make discoveries, you will see emulation spreading among you. (Gouges, 1789: 13)

He tells them that through emulation they will acquire better, more useful skills and techniques, which will ensure their survival. But they will also acquire habits derived from their joint work and collaboration, which will lead them to care for each other when they are old or sick.

We might liken Gouges's idea of the primitive community to a modern science lab, in which scientists and students work alongside each other, hoping to make a breakthrough, competing with each other in the sense that one student's assiduity will move the others to work harder, but not doing anything that puts an experiment at risk or that might slow down the eventual discovery. Of course, not all scientific labs are free of harmful competition, and no doubt science suffers from it, but the fact that scientists are able to work together to bring about new ideas does suggest that Gouges was right about the benefits of emulation.

In the second chapter of *Primitive Happiness*, Gouges proposes an experiment that would demonstrate that she is right that natural emulation will lead any primitive human society to progress. She suggests men and women with speech disabilities should be given the care of orphaned newborns and bring them up in complete isolation from the rest of the world, in a fertile land surrounded by high walls, to which no one but those responsible for the experiment would have access. Gouges believed that this would help demonstrate the way in which emulation helps primitive societies develop:

> I am persuaded that as soon as fifteen years have passed, we will begin to make discoveries about those people, living apart from civilized society; very useful discoveries, I say. We would have to let them be free in their inclinations as well as in their emulation, leaving nature to act entirely, and able to recognize what she would create nowadays... (Gouges, 1789: 33)

It is difficult to understand what she expects we would find beyond the walls, fifteen years later. She starts from the assumption that the children would find themselves to be superior to their parents. But would they develop a language of their own? Would they seek to communicate at all with their parents by learning to sign with them? She does not assume that all will be well – she admits that some savages are both fierce and incapable of thinking ahead, but she adds that the same is true of civilized people. This suggests that Gouges is making an important pedagogical point here: what the experiment shows is that emulation without instruction will tend to the same rates of success and failure on average than we can expect in civilized societies. Nature may grant one or more of the children an insight that will help them advance, just as happens in the civilized world, but without the bad effects of instruction, or schooling for the sake of social advancement, which, as we saw earlier, she regards as one of the principal causes of inequality and poverty.

This subsection began with the observation that the downfall of human societies, according to Rousseau, that began with the competitiveness that made us enemies to one another, was to be found in the performing arts. Gouges, while she disagrees with Rousseau about the place of emulation in human progress, agrees with him about the harmful effects of some forms of entertainments, which are designed to make the rich spend more and entice the poor to drown their troubles rather than seek to resolve them if they can. She lists in particular any places where drinking, gambling, and prostitution take place. But this does not, as far as she is concerned, include the arts when they are performed as art, rather than mere amusement. The theatre has always been, she points out, the most ennobling form of amusement for people, one which even the Greeks used to educate, as well as entertain. This is set out in chapter five of *Primitive Happiness*, the chapter preceding her proposal for theatrical reform:

> To correct various abuses, to entirely destroy the excesses of luxury, to abolish an infinite number of public gaming houses, and create amusements that lift the soul of the French and purify courage; to clean the streets of Paris from prostitutes … Whatever reform can be made in the Kingdom, the French require distraction. All peoples, even the most savage, have sought amusement, but the most noble and pure are those that have lasted the longest: such as the famous tournaments in Europe; the good theatres of the Greek, that still delight us today. But the taste has gone and a revolution is needed to return the French to their true character. Preserve the arts, and rein in the excesses of luxury; abolish, mercilessly, a half of all performances; create one that can purify manners, make prejudice disappear, and become the source of a noble emulation and usefulness to Society. (Gouges, 1789: 67–9)

There is, Gouges believed, real power in the theatre to improve character while serving the necessary role of entertainment. And this improvement takes place through emulation, because emulation involves, necessarily, a kind of imitation, which in the case of the theatre is the imitation of human behaviour.

Rousseau recognizes the place of imitation in the theatre, but he does not believe that it goes beyond mere entertainment: 'Let no one then attribute to the theatre the power to change sentiments or morals [manners] which it can only follow or embellish. An author would brave the general taste would soon write for himself alone' (Rousseau, 1968: 19).

Theatre can imitate, but only superficially, only what it sees, and if it wants to be successful, it should imitate only the traits that the public admires in itself. This means, according to Rousseau, that the theatre can play no pedagogical or improving role. (One should note the incongruity of Rousseau believing this, given that his immense popularity was grounded at least in part in his propensity to show off his readers' bad habits.) But another powerful reason for Rousseau to distrust the theatre was the central role that women, as actresses, played in it. In *Emile* he explained that women were naturally unable to control their sexual urges, and that this meant chastity had to be imposed on them in order to keep peace in society (Rousseau, 1979: 359).[9] According to Rousseau, the theatre took away the constraints on women to behave, and as such represented a great threat.

It is useful to bring up the extent to which Gouges and Rousseau disagree about this. For Gouges, what is wrong with the theatre is that women do not play a strong enough role in it, and to the extent that they do participate, as actresses or spectators, their actions are determined by the male expectation that actresses should be loose women, not by their own moral decisions.

Gouges then notes an apparently unrelated problem: women, she says, are underutilized. They have a potential to be useful for society that is not taken into account, so that instead of aiding the progress of society, they slow it down. But rather than blame women for their impact on progress, she portrays it as an injustice being done to them:

> Should not women, for example, . . . receive some marks of encouragement, when by their merit and honor they elevate their sex? Don't women make up half of society? And unfortunately, their lack of emulation contributes to the ruin of the other half. (Gouges, 1789: 68)

Women, she says, if they receive suitable encouragement and emulation, can be useful to society. Moreover, her own experience dictates that one way in which they can be of use is through writing for the theatre. Women, she says, are capable of writing plays that are aesthetically pleasing but also suitable in terms

---

[9] On Rousseau, women, and the theatre, see Pateman (1980).

of moral content, that is, unlikely to lead spectators to further depravation. Gouges often uses her own experience as evidence, noting that she has herself written enough plays to keep a theatre going for a good few years. All her own plays are certainly led by a desire for moral reforms, and desire to help the oppressed, whether women or slaves. But why should women's theatre be morally superior to men's theatre? Perhaps Gouges is thinking of eighteenth-century men's and women's motivations in writing for the theatre. A man may write simply because it is a way in which he knows he can make a living. He may be a good writer, but one who, as Rousseau suggests, will use his skills to please and to sell, rather than to improve his audience. Why does Gouges assume that putting on women's plays would result in moral improvement? Close reading of *Primitive Happiness* suggests that, rather than presuming a natural moral superiority of women, she believes that women playwrights will bring improvement for two reasons. First, having a larger number of plays to choose from will make it more likely that morally worthy plays can be found. Gouges knows that among women's writings, some are morally superior – she includes her own in that category. Second, she argues that bringing women authors into competition with men will bring about a different kind of competition, and 'different competition would uplift women's souls and make men more polite, more genuine, and more considerate' (Gouges, 1789: 79). She cites her friend and playwright Mercier as an example of a male writer who has benefitted from friendly competition with a female writer (herself), and whose plays are an example of 'true sentiment and heartbreaking drama' (Gouges, 1789: 79).

Primitive Happiness uses Gouges's conclusions on the role of emulation in early human progress and the relationship between emulation and the arts to propose a cure for the social degeneration both she and Rousseau have observed. The arts, she says, can be used to bring us back to a state where we work together towards human progress. Concretely, her proposal concerns that which Rousseau felt was most harmful: women and the theatre. Gouges, who agrees that European theatre, and in particular Parisian theatre, in the late eighteenth century is not a healthy representative of the arts but a space where decadence is praised and encouraged, argues that it must be reformed, and this reform must come from those who supposedly most care about human progress: the state, meaning, in 1788, the king. Thus, she drafts a proposal addressed to the king for a new, state-funded theatre: 'The National Theatre, or the Women's Theatre' (Gouges, 1789: 71).

This theatre will promote real artistic genius instead of pandering to the rich. And the best way of finding genius to promote, she says, it to look for a previously untapped, and hence uncorrupted, source: women writers.

> A great number of well-born women are ruined because men, who have
> seized everything for themselves, have prevented women from elevating
> themselves, and obtaining for themselves useful and lasting resources. Why
> should my sex not one day be rescued from this thoughtlessness to which
> their lack of emulation exposes them? Women have always written. They
> have been allowed to contend with men in the theatrical profession. But they
> would need proof of greater encouragement. Such is my plan.
>
> (Gouges, 1789: 72)

But actors, as well as writers, must be found, and existing actors are not
a source of virtue, Gouges knows. Gouges notes that among the complaints (the
doléances) presented to the king in preparation for the meeting of the Estates,
a recurring one was that the rich spent too much of their time at the theatre. The
complaint is not that they see plays, but that the kind of entertainment they
pursue is fundamentally immoral, involving prostitution, gambling, and infidelity, and that it shows a complete lack of concern for those who suffer from
poverty while at the same time working to feed the leisure of the rich (Gouges,
1789: 67–8). Not only are the pleasures of the rich frivolous, empty of content,
and sometimes downright immoral, they also encourage prejudice, says
Gouges. For a play to be performed it has to be accepted by the all-powerful
company of actors, who then decide when, how often, and in what way it will be
performed. In order to persuade actors to take on a play, many authors, Gouges
tells us, have to compromise their artistic and moral integrity. Those authors
who refuse to give in to the actors' capricious demands do not have their plays
staged. Some of these authors, Gouges says, are women, and all would benefit
from a theatrical outlet that was not dominated by actors and that produced
plays chosen for their quality, rather than the bribes or favours that came with
them.

The solution, she argues, is to create a school for actors, as part of the new
theatre. The school will take in talented youngsters from impoverished but
respectable middle-class families, provide them with a well-rounded,
humanities-based education, and offer them the possibility of a career as an
actor. Even if they turn down a career as an actor, their education will enable
them to pursue other careers.

Gouges thus seeks to apply fully the concept of emulation stated at the
beginning of *Primitive Happiness*, in the dying elder's speech. Emulation is
a tool for progress, but that progress is fundamentally social progress, enabling
human beings to live and flourish together, which implies that they must care for
each other. Her theatrical project is not merely one designed to improve the
theatre, or at least prevent it from causing the sort of harm Rousseau imagines it
might cause; the project also promotes social justice: it offers women

employment that will make full use of their capacity, without holding them back simply because they are women. It will also help educate those children whose families want them educated but cannot afford it. Note that Gouges is not promoting universal education. In *Primitive Happiness*, and indeed elsewhere (in Section 4 we will recognize this in her views on the education of slaves and masters in *Zamore and Mirza*), she argues that the wrong education can be a negative force in society in that it distracts people from the work that truly matters. Why should someone who tills the land leave the countryside to study law? Or worse, study in order to speak and present as someone educated, only to become a valet or a maid to an aristocrat? Education, she believes, can distract from happiness, and should be handled with care. But the wrong kind of education also becomes a form of domination, or a tool for some members of society to dominate others, at the same time as it creates an illusion of equality. We will bear this in mind as we focus, in the following two sections, on Gouges's accounts of liberty and equality – the two standards of the French Revolution.

3 Liberty

3.1 Republicanism and Domination

French Revolution thinkers, including Gouges, tended to be republicans rather than democrats. Both terms were derived from ancient philosophy. Democracy was unpopular because of its association with Athens: it brought to mind an obsolete system of Greek government that was only possible in city states (Monnier, 1999: 52–3; Scurr, 2013: 2). Republicanism represented a richer and broader tradition. Also originating with the Greeks, it had been established in Roman times by political thinkers such as Livy, Cato, Cicero, and Plutarch, later reinstated by Machiavelli, and again revived in seventeenth-century England with Harrington, Needham, and Sydney.[10]

Eighteenth-century French republicanism, while not essentially distinct from that of England in the previous century, had its own specific features, some adapted from Roman republicanism, some drawing on seventeenth-century British political thought, some from the American Revolution, and some specific to France. While this doesn't amount to a well-defined set of principles, there were nonetheless important commonalities to be found among the proponents of republicanism in eighteenth-century France. These commonalities can be summed up as follows: first, French revolutionary republicans wanted to

---

[10] This is the 'received' history of republicanism, but Manjeet Ramgotra (2014) has suggested that the three writers were in fact going in different directions and perhaps should not be taken to represent a tradition.

theorize social relationships of freedom as independence or non-domination; second, they saw republicanism as a virtue-led politics; and finally, they embraced a conceptualization of political participation that was not essentially democratic and did not necessarily depend on the universal vote (Bergès, 2019a).

The primary characteristic of French revolutionary republican thought is the claim that citizens must be free from domination, that is, they must not be governed in such a way that a ruler may arbitrarily effect changes to the course of their lives. While freedom from domination was equally important for the likes of Harrington, Needham, and Sydney, or indeed Cato, Livy, and Cicero, the way in which it was conceived during the French Revolution was somewhat different. Domination was observed not merely in the relations between aristocratic men and their king or ruler but also in other layers of society. Indeed, the domination of the poor by the rich that was enabled and encouraged by aristocratic privileges was among the first injustices to be questioned, and the abolition of privileges was proposed less than three weeks after the fall of the Bastille, on the night of 4 August 1789, thus establishing the first principles of the new Constitution. But while this interest in the dominated status of non-aristocrats was in itself fairly radical, the French Revolution also questioned the domination of slaves and women. While these debates did not result in much more than proposals for reforms of abolition that were turned down and new divorce laws that lasted for less than a decade, they nonetheless opened the public debate on the position of slaves and women. Gouges was an important part of these debates, as we will see in this section and the next.

French revolutionaries did not always conceive of the outcome of the revolution as a republic, and even once that thought set in, it did not necessarily translate to democracy. A king could lead a republic as long as that king was not a tyrant, was accountable to the public, and was motivated by the common good. If such a king could be appointed, then one plausible republican set-up would be the constitutional monarchy, modelled on the English government and aspects of the mixed governments described by Cicero and Machiavelli. At the beginning of the Revolution, many republicans, including Gouges and the Abbé Sieyès, supported a constitutional monarchy (Hont, 2005: 132).

It was only after the king's attempted escape from Paris, in the summer of 1791, that republicans turned to more radical ideas and government models that did not include a king, even one with dramatically reduced powers. But even then, the idea of a republican constitution without a monarch was a hard sell for a country that had only ever known monarchy. For this reason, the Condorcet couple, Nicolas and Sophie, together with Thomas Paine and a few others, decided to publish a journal entitled *Le Républican* in which they would print articles explaining what republicanism was to the French public. The authors of the *Républican* appealed to the Roman conception of liberty as independence, arguing that the French people could not be free while a king ruled over them in virtue of hereditary and arbitrary powers. While the king may not be malevolent, they argued, his descendant could be (Bergès, 2015: 103; Condorcet and Paine, 1991: 8,9, 14). They also compared the French people to children who could not mature while they lived under a monarch, even if that monarch ruled together with an assembly (Bergès, 2015: 108). Only a full republic, they said, would enable the French to attain the freedom they wanted.

What was Gouges's political alignment? The answer is complex, and I will develop it in the third subsection. I will show that she was not, as is often supposed, a monarchist, or even, like Germaine de Staël, a committed constitutional monarchist. But she was not a die-hard republican either, in the way that Madame Roland and Sophie de Grouchy were. Although she was closer to the Girondins than any other group of revolutionary politicians – mostly because they were committed to abolitionism and women's rights – she did not go in for party politics. Gouges described herself as a republican, but her view evolved during her career as a political writer, starting in 1788, just before the Revolution, and finishing with her death at the beginning of the Terror. She started off in favour of a republican monarchy, then agreed that the monarchy should be abolished (but not by killing the king), and finally proposed that the form of government for France should be decided democratically, even if that meant the return of the monarchy.

Although she came to believe there was no longer a place in France for a king or a royal family, at first Gouges was somewhat sceptical that the French people would achieve the necessary maturity needed to rule themselves and therefore achieve freedom through independence. Like many revolutionary thinkers, including Jacques-Pierre Brissot and Maximilien Robespierre, she believed that independence required virtue, and that virtue could only come slowly and with effort. She would have agreed with Kant that acquiring the capacity to think for oneself takes time and work, and most people, left to themselves, are more likely to fall back into lazy habits of letting themselves be guided by masters, clergy, or rulers. As Kant wrote five years before the French Revolution started:

> [A] public can achieve enlightenment only slowly. A revolution may bring about the end of a personal despotism or of avaricious tyrannical oppression, but never a true reform of modes of thought. New prejudices will serve, in place of the old, as guide lines for the unthinking multitude.
>
> (Kant, 1991: 55)

For Gouges, as we will see in the coming subsections, the lack of maturity of the new French citizens, or 'democrats', as she called them, was what the Revolution had failed to tackle, and it manifested itself in an inability to live with newly acquired liberty. She also insisted, later in the Revolution, that any liberty gained would be lost without virtue, not only in the case of the people, but especially of the leaders. On the other hand, as we will see, she did not believe that maturity or virtue would require a complete re-education of the population of France, but thought that it could be achieved through the example of leaders. As we saw in the previous section, Gouges thought that virtue was a natural state which could be lost and regained through emulation. Men and women of primitive societies were virtuous until they were confronted with a couple who appeared to be superior to them. Then, emulation and the desire to become equal to these apparently superior people led to a disconnect with their essentially virtuous nature. Later in *Primitive Happiness*, Gouges argues that part of the way to re-establish virtue is to do away with luxurious displays of superiority and instead to model virtue to the public though the theatre. Here we will see how she believed the same principle could be applied to revolutionary France by having its leaders model virtue.

3.2 Liberty and Virtue

In 1790, the Minister of Finance, Jacques Necker, whose earlier dismissal in July 1789 had prompted a young journalist, Camille Desmoulins, to climb on a café table and call for the Parisians to take arms, was dismissed again. He decided that a self-imposed exile was needed to preserve his and his family's lives, and in September he left France for his Swiss home of Coppet. Olympe de Gouges too was ready to leave France – her play on slavery, *Zamore and Mirza*, had been badly received, heckled by the colonists, and cancelled by the actors after a three-day run. She wanted to take it to London, where she expected abolitionism to find more sympathy. Gouges did not, in fact, leave Paris, but she recorded her intention to do so in a pamphlet entitled *M. Necker and Madame de Gouges's Departure or Madame de Gouges's Farewells to the French and to M. Necker* (Gouges, 1790a). The central argument of the pamphlet is that although both Necker and herself had done their best to serve the cause of liberty in France, that had not been enough. The people who had once been oppressed had become oppressors themselves:

> I loathe the avariciousness of the clergy; I detest the ostentation of the nobility; both have brought about our downfall but by imitating them we will lose them and ourselves. (Gouges, 1790a).

The point of the revolution, Gouges thought, was not simply for power to change hands but for it to be wielded better. And as far as she could see, the people of France did not have what it took to wield power fairly. This is something she had witnessed early on during riots, when 'five hundred to a thousand' people would gang up to 'butcher a single defenseless citizen' (Gouges, 1790a). But whereas she might have been prepared to forgive the act of enraged, recently liberated crowds against those they perceived to be their oppressors, she did not feel the same about individuals abusing their newly acquired liberty. Those who behaved recklessly because of the revolution would soon revert to their status as subjects: they did not have the inner resources to remain republican citizens. In the second half of the *Farewell to Necker*, she relates an anecdote in which such a reversal happens. Having witnessed a coach driver insulting a national guard, she challenged his patriotic spirit. The driver replied that he had had enough of being treated poorly by arrogant guards who thought they needn't pay for transport in virtue of their status as revolutionary heroes. He added that as a result he was even poorer now than before the revolution and concluded:

> I was a proper democrat from the start of the revolution, believing it would do
> us good but I'm now a dogged aristocrat (Gouges, 1790a).

If the coach driver was honest about his reversal of allegiance, the guards presented an even greater danger to liberty, Gouges thought, because they attributed to themselves the status of masters, taking what they wanted without thinking of those they hurt in the process. Gouges herself was later a victim of such post-revolutionary arrogance, when she was threatened by a driver who wanted to overcharge her. She relates the incident in the Postscript to the *Rights of Woman*:

> I threatened him with the law; he said he cared nothing for it and insisted that
> I pay him for two hours. We arrived at a justice of the peace, whom I shall
> generously not name, although the authoritarian way he dealt with me merits
> a formal denunciation. No doubt he was unaware that the woman asking for
> justice was the authoress of so many charitable and equitable works. Paying
> no attention to my reasons he pitilessly condemned me to pay the coachman
> what he demanded. Knowing the law better than he did I said to him, 'Sir,
> I refuse and I would beg you to be aware that you are exceeding the preroga-
> tive of your position.' So this man, or to put it better this lunatic, got carried
> away and threatened me with La Force [prison]. (Gouges, 1791)

Gouges saw that the reversal of power, instead of bringing democracy, could turn unprepared members of the lower classes, especially men, into petty tyrants who simply replicated the harmful behaviour of those they had toppled. And, in the *Farewell to Necker*, she argued that such reversal would eventually effect a counter-revolution:

> I announce to all my fellow citizens, on behalf of common sense, that this counter-revolution may perhaps take place, but with no civil war, without the efforts of the foreign powers and that it will take place naturally, of its own accord, at least in part if not in its entirety, and by the force of circumstance, especially if all the French carry on as they have been for another six months, destroying and rebuilding nothing; everyone wants to command, no one obeys; everything is wrecked; everything is in a deplorable disorder; their passion for liberty is still turning the heads of the French. But once this passion is gone I hope they will recognise that a single master is more useful to men that if all men were masters all together. (Gouges, 1790a)

So what would need to change, according to Gouges, for the Revolution to be successful? It would have to be the case that its actors developed 'an upright soul, a disinterested heart' (Gouges, 1790a). Her concerns that the souls of the French were not ready for the success of the Revolution was shared by many of her contemporaries – though perhaps none expressed it as clearly or as early on as she did. Jacques-Pierre Brissot, who had travelled to America before the Revolution and published his notes in 1791, noted that what kept the Americans safe from a counter-revolution, and what made their republic work, was their morals. To act moderately, virtuously, and always in accordance with reason was key, he said, to a successful republic. And while the French did not need to learn how to become free, they would do well to copy the Americans if they wanted to remain so: 'We have no need to learn from Americans how to attain the blessing of liberty', he wrote in the preface to *Voyage*, 'but we have to learn from them the secret of preserving it' (Brissot, 1791).

Gouges's and Brissot's worry about French people's fitness for freedom touches on a larger debate that was started earlier by Rousseau and Catharine Macaulay and continued by Wollstonecraft and others: in order to be free, one must first be educated. But how can we ensure that a dominated people should be educated to be free? Rousseau (1979: 49) and Macaulay (1790: 170) both saw the answer in private education: it is parents' duty to seek tutors for their children that will teach them to think for themselves, so that they may not inherit the prejudices that impede social progress. Mary Wollstonecraft thought that there were sufficient numbers of educated people in England and France to start planning for a general reform of state education, and in the dedication of her *Vindication of the Rights of Woman*, she enjoins Talleyrand, then in charge of education in France, not to forget to include women in his programme, as a half-educated nation can only go round in circles, not progress (Wollstonecraft, 2014: 22).

What was Gouges's position? While she believed virtue needed to be established in France in order for liberty to take the place of domination, she did not think that education was the way to bring this about. As we saw in the previous section, Gouges believed that virtue was a human being's natural inclination but that it could be perverted by poor social arrangements that privileged luxury and personal advancement, instead of collaboration for the good of all. Emulation, she feels, not education, is both the way to regain virtue and to maintain it. She suggested in *Primitive Happiness* that the theatre could play that role: encouraging the French public to be virtuous by putting on virtuous plays, acted by virtuous actors. Gouges believed that in the context of the Revolution, it was no longer actors and plays the public must turn to (although she still thought that those had a role to play, in particular when it came to changing public perception about slavery) but political leaders. They should lead through example, manifesting their own virtue in all their acts. This was also a way of marking the break with the old regime: the rulers of the old regime were not virtuous – their dissipation had sunk France into debt. The new leaders had to be exemplary in their virtue.

There were two popular arguments for replacing the king with elected citizens. The first was about sovereignty, in that the nation had to be the source of its own law in order to be free. But the second was a direct reflection on the king and his entourage, who were seen as lacking in virtue and wallowing in expensive and criminal debauchery. The queen, especially, had been the object of attacks: she was said to be spending the kingdom's money on clothes and jewels for herself and her entourage, throwing expensive parties, and taking numerous lovers, both male and female. The king's own expenses had also been revealed in part to the public when his finance minister, Necker, had published his 'Account to the King' in 1781. The new order of elected citizens, by contrast, took care to present themselves as virtuous, and in particular, temperate. They were men who claimed to put the interests of the nation ahead of their own, to be honest and transparent in their transactions, and uninterested in the pursuit of personal gain. In particular, Robespierre 'the incorruptible', Roland 'the virtuous', and Brissot, founder of a journal called *The Patriot*, gained the people's trust in virtue of their exemplary moral character. Danton was the exception that confirmed the rule: his perceived love for the nation and his charismatic appeal made up for his obvious lack of temperance. It was customary for politicians to show off their own and their friends' virtue, and show off their enemies' lack of it. All had been brought up on Roman republican texts and sought to model themselves on republican heroes such as Cato. The nation came first, and everything personal, including the well-being of their family, second (Linton, 2013: 37).

A good revolutionary republican needed to demonstrate that they lived their lives according to Roman or even Spartan virtues. When Robespierre accused Brissot, and with him the entire Girondins party, of political plotting, Brissot responded by arguing that he had no personal ambition and that he and his family lived in relative poverty (Linton, 2013: 275).

Another example of Girondist virtue is that of Marie-Jeanne Phlipon Roland, wife of 'the virtuous' Roland, minister of the interior, and an influential member of the Girondin group in her own right. 'Manon' Roland's participation in revolutionary politics took place in her home, where she hosted dinner parties for members of the government and their friends. In order to prevent her dinner parties from becoming the object of political gossip, she made sure never to invite women (because this might have led her enemies to accuse her of running a brothel) and to serve only simple one-course meals, with sugared water instead of alcohol (Roland, 1827: 402). Manon Roland also attempted to demonstrate her allegiance to Roman virtue by behaving as she thought a good matron would, always sitting apart during those dinners and working at a piece of embroidery while she listened silently (Roland, 1902: 268).

While Olympe de Gouges, unlike Brissot and Roland, was not classically educated, we know from references she makes in her pamphlets that she was familiar with some of the classics of Roman republicanism. We also know that she too was very keen to establish herself as a virtuous citizen, although not necessarily, unlike Roland, as a virtuous *female* citizen. As we saw in Section 1.3, Gouges's views on gender were ambiguous. She relied on her experience as a woman, but she did not argue that feminine character traits were part of an essential nature. In the *Rights of Woman* (1791), she argues that the sort of virtues developed by couples, or parents, were beneficial to the republic. Therefore, her experience as a mother as well as her experience as a political writer were both relevant to her worth as a citizen.

In the autumn of 1792, at the outset of the Terror, Gouges challenged Robespierre to show whether he was in fact as virtuous as she was. She said that she was prepared to sacrifice her life for the republic: was he?

> Robespierre! Have you the courage to imitate me? I suggest we two take a bath in the Seine, but in order to wash away all the stains you have acquired since the 10th, we will attach cannonballs of sixteen or twenty-four to our feet; then, together, we will rush headlong into the flow. Your death will calm minds, and the sacrifice of [my] pure life will disarm the heavens. I am useful to my country, as you know, but your death will at least free it of its greatest scourge, and maybe I will never have served it better: I am capable of such extreme patriotism. Such is the courage of the great characters that you yourself describe without ever knowing any. 'One can outrage virtue, but memory lives on

forever,' you are right. 'The small-minded and facetious never last, only the great live on.' It is too marvellous that you yourself should write their defence and your proper accusation! Mediocre and boastful compared to your superiors in merit and talent; a cringing impostor to the people: there is your portrait. Tell me, what, actually, will be your place in the pages of history; lift up your eyes, if you dare, and see the ideal philosopher and people's magistrate.

(Gouges, 1792c)

The context of the challenge is as follows. In November 1792, the Girondins had accused Robespierre of attempting to take over the government through his role as leader of the Paris Commune. Robespierre had responded by appealing to Roman history, mocking his accusers for mixing their Roman history references (did they think he was trying to become a dictator, a tribune, or set up a triumvirate?), and justifying his actions by comparing himself to Cicero, who, when he stopped Catiline's conspiracy, went above the law. He had concluded that what the Revolution most needed was a virtuous leader who could, if need be, do what Cicero did: act above the law, but only a leader of exceptional virtue could take on this role (Robespierre, 1792). This speech was made in the wake of two massacres: that of the king's private guards on 10 August and that of imprisoned members of the clergy and of the aristocracy at the beginning of September. Gouges responded by challenging Robespierre's virtue. How could a leader responsible, at least in part, for the deaths of August and September 1792, the attacks on the king's Swiss Guards in the Tuileries, and the massacres of prisoners dragged out of their cells and summarily executed in the streets call himself virtuous?

Gouges accused Robespierre of faking his virtue in order to assume power. If he was not a Cicero, then acting above the law made him nothing but a tyrant and a danger to the republic. If Robespierre had sufficient virtue to recognize that he had become a danger to the republic he meant to protect, he ought, she argued, to remove himself from the equation. To make it easier, and at the same time prove that she was virtuous and acting only for the good of the nation, she would join him in death.

3.3 Liberty and the People's Choice

Gouges started her career as a political writer on the royalist side. Then she became a constitutional monarchist, and later again, a republican. This is by no means unusual. Very few revolutionary writers started off as republicans or anti-monarchists (Sophie de Grouchy and Manon Roland were notable exceptions). For most revolutionaries, the republic only became a realistic option after the king's flight and his capture in Varennes in June 1791. Even then, some were not convinced: Robespierre, according to Manon Roland, was nervous and wondering whether republicanism could make sense for France, and Etienne Dumont, a friend of Condorcet, withdrew his support from the journal *Le Républicain* as soon as the king came back to Paris, arguing it made more sense now to have a constitutional monarchy (Bergès, 2015: 106; Dumont, 1832: 333).

Gouges's allegiance to the king and queen is evident in her earlier writings. In 1788, she anticipated a happy result from the gathering of the Estates, a result brought about by the king and queen's good will and genuine interest in the happiness of the people of France:

> Sitting on the Throne, adored by the most virtuous man and the best of Kings, her generous compassion will allow her to come forward and succour the unfortunate; she will constantly support the elderly, deprived of strength, shelter and basic needs and console widows and orphans.
>
> Oh all-powerful Queen! And you King of the French, you have been given a feeble account of the ills of your People; their pains, their sufferings, their miseries have been painted in favourable colours. People avoid burdening you yet, in order to ease the suffering of your subjects, you must be burdened by their troubles. (Gouges, 1788c)

The praise of the king and queen is followed by a plan for a luxury tax, which, building on the success of the voluntary tax she had proposed two months earlier (Gouges, 1788b), would help relieve the national debt. Then Gouges describes a dream in which she sees the (slightly fantastic) effect of reforms brought about by the king having read and responded to all the grievances submitted to him. The world she sees in her dream is free of sickness and poverty, and the clean, safe streets are filled with happy people wearing comfortable, non-luxurious clothing.

Three years later, following the king's attempted escape from France, Gouges addressed her *Rights of Woman* to the queen. This text was published at the same time as the king ratified the new Constitution, and so coincides with the short period when France was a constitutional monarchy. The tone is now different. Rather than simply praising the queen, she also emphasizes that she speaks to her in liberty, as an equal, not as a servant to a master or a subject to a tyrant:

> My aim is to speak to you freely: I did not wait for the era of Liberty to express myself thus but showed the same determination at a time when blind Despots punished such noble audacity. (Gouges, 1791)

Gouges still recognizes the queen's influence, but wants to make it known that her allegiance has changed. A year later, in September 1792, when France was proclaimed a republic, Gouges claimed her allegiance to it:

I have never vacillated in my opinions and yet, in the last four years we have had three Governments. That of the Republic is no doubt my element.

(Gouges, 1792b)

Clearly, she moved with the times, and was ever keen to help political progress. Lest we think of her as an opportunistic turncoat, however, it is worth noting that even as a republican she did not hesitate to challenge power. In particular, she was ever ready to criticize revolutionary leaders, including Robespierre and Marat, and accused them of anti-republican violence:

And Marat? Marat! A true agitator, destroyer of Laws, mortal enemy of order, of humanity, of his motherland, accused and convicted of wanting to introduce a dictatorship into France, and of ceaselessly threatening to bring about the complete dissolution of the National Convention, Marat lives in freedom in the society of which he is the tyrant and the plague.

(Gouges, 1792b)

However, her republicanism did not mean that she was ready to turn a blind eye on what was done to the king. When, in December 1792, the king was arrested and taken to trial, at the risk of being taken for a royalist, Gouges offered her services as his advocate. She argued that while the king had harmed the nation by his very existence, he was guilty as king, and once that title had been abolished, so would the guilt:

As king, I believe Louis to be in the wrong, but take away this proscribed title and he ceases to be guilty, in the eyes of the republic.

Does Louis the Last threaten the republic more than his brothers, or his son? His brothers are still united with the foreign powers and only work on their own behalf. Louis Capet's son is innocent, and will survive his father.

Louis Capet's greatest crime, it must be conceded, was to be born a king at a time when philosophy was silently laying the foundations of the republic.

(Gouges, 1792d)

When Louis Capet, stripped of his title, was found guilty of high treason, Gouges published a second pamphlet, a "Decree of Death against Louis Capet, presented by Olympe de Gouges," in which she argued that he ought not to be put to death by the nation, as this would present a risk to the republic:

Louis dead will still enslave the Universe. Louis alive will break the chains of the Universe by smashing the sceptres of his equals. If they resist? Well! Let a noble despair immortalize us. It has been said, with reason, that our situation is neither like that of the English nor the Romans. I have a great example to offer posterity; here it is: Louis' son is innocent, but he could be a pretender to the crown and I would like to deny him all pretension. Therefore I would like Louis, his wife,

his children and all his family to be chained in a carriage and driven into
the heart of our armies, between the enemy fire and our own artillery.

(Gouges, 1793a)

Her argument appeals to a then well-known fact about the workings of monarchy: the king cannot die. As soon as one holder of the title dies, the next king
rises. The immortality of the king was such an important precept that
a Chancelier, when a monarch died, could not wear mourning.

Despite Gouges's best efforts, on 15 January, Louis Capet was found guilty
by an overwhelming majority of the 749 deputies. Two days later, 346 deputies
voted for the death penalty. On 21 January 1793, he was guillotined.

Gouges persevered in her argument that the king's execution would harm
the republic. She noted the inconsistency in trying Louis as a man for crimes
committed as a king. Killing the man for the crimes of the king only perpetuated the title. The real death of Louis XVI was the abolition of monarchy. The
man who survived it was no more than an ordinary citizen who could not have
the power to do the harm he was being tried for. His dramatic death only
meant that his supporters perceive him as having died a king and pass the title
on to his heir. This is indeed what happened with the restoration of the
monarchy in the nineteenth century, with the title being passed on to
Louis's brothers, Louis XVIII and Charles X, the Count of Provence and
the Count of Artois.

In *The Three Urns*, published six months after Louis's death, Gouges reiter-
ated her argument, adding premises from the history of the Roman republic:

Oh French, what has caused your dissension? The death of the tyrant? Well,
he is dead! All factions must fall with his head and, despite myself, your
extravagant criminality recalls to my mind the panoply of great revolutions:
I place it before your eyes; dare to observe it.

The Syracusans having dethroned their tyrant told him to flee far from their
shores, or stay and become their equal; they allowed him to be master of his
fate, the chap obeyed his sovereign and became a schoolteacher. The Roman
republic chased out the Tarquins. In vain did they attempt to arm their tyrannical friends against a people who wanted freedom; they died itinerant vaga-
bonds. The English, whom you try so hard to *mimic*, sent Charles I to the
scaffold. This historic act of justice could not free them from tyranny for the
dying Charles perpetuated royalty in England. Alas, oh French, such is our
actual state: Louis Capet is dead, yet Louis Capet still reigns among us. Stop
pretending it is not so, it is time for the mask to fall and for each of you to freely
pronounce, openly, if you do or do not want a republic. It is time to put a stop to
this cruel war that has only swallowed up your treasure and harvested the most
brilliant of your young. Blood, alas, has flowed far too freely!

Spouting republicanism with hearts full of royalism, you arm region
against region little caring about the denouement of this bloody drama.

> Despite seeing the thoughtlessness and imprudence of your horrible dissimu-
> lation I still want to serve you and save you. (Gouges, 1793c)

The claim that killing Louis endangered the republic is perhaps clearer in this
text. Had Louis done what the Syracusan tyrant did, and gone on to lead the life
of a regular citizen, he might have lived long enough for the republic to become
established and thoughts of his succession extinguished. But not only did the
execution make the eventual transmission of his title inevitable, it also showed
a certain amount of doubt among the republicans that monarchy had truly been
abolished. Later on in the pamphlet, she built on this doubt and asked that the
French people should vote to decide which form of government they truly
wanted: republic, federation, or constitutional monarchy. This was perceived
as a direct attack on Robespierre, as under his leadership the Paris Commune
had more or less usurped the convention, in which sat representatives of the
whole of France. Even if the French chose to remain a republic, her text implied,
Robespierre and the commune would have no part in its government.

> Several *départements* are rising up in favour of federalism; the royalists are
> strong both in and out of the country; the constitutional government, one and
> indivisible, is in a courageous minority. Blood flows everywhere, this strug-
> gle is appalling and dreadful in my view. It is time for the combat to cease.
> I would like the Convention to express the spirit of the Decree that I will
> dictate to you. … All the *départements* must be enjoined to convoke
> primary assemblies: three urns must be placed on the President of the
> assembly's table, each one labelled with one of the following inscrip-
> tions: *republican Government, one and indivisible; federal Government;*
> *monarchic Government.*
> …A civic celebration will accompany this solemnity; this sensitive and
> decisive act will calm passions and destroy factions … the rebels will
> disperse themselves; the enemy powers will ask for peace; the universe, as
> surprised in its admiration as it was attentive, for so long, to the dissension in
> France, will cry out: the French are invincible! (Gouges, 1793c)

The conclusion Gouges draws may seem somewhat paradoxical as it suggests
that the people's right to choose their own government should be put to the vote.
At least, should they settle for constitutional monarchy, they would take a step
back as far as gaining voting power was concerned. The years after the revolution saw at first a gradual increase in the number of French people who were
allowed to vote. Members of the Legislative Assembly were elected in 1791 by
the first public vote. However, only those male citizens who paid taxes corres-
ponding to a week's labour were allowed to vote. The National Convention,
elected a year later, expanded the voting population by allowing all working
Frenchmen aged twenty-one or over, domiciled for a year at their address, to

vote. It is unlikely that a return to monarchy at this point would have further extended the vote. The point of a monarch, after all, was to concentrate the decision-making power, not to spread it out further.

Gouges, while she was hoping that the vote would continue to be extended until it included at least women, and perhaps the non-white population of the French colonies, did not believe that democracy could be imposed on an unwilling and unprepared people. And certainly, the Parisian triumvirate – Robespierre, Danton, and Marat – could not impose their violence on the people of the provinces. These people, she concluded, should be asked, while it was still possible for them to vote, what they wanted.

Gouges's *Three Urns* presages a thought about democracy that reflects what later thinkers have said about it, including Philip Pettit, who noted this paradox in the theory of democratic government: a people may choose democratically to be ruled undemocratically:

> A society that makes decisions on a democratic basis, with everyone sharing equally in control of government, could in principle decide on a permanent renunciation of democratic rule, denying future generations the right to shape their institutions on an equally shared basis. (Pettit, 2012: 25).

Going back from being a republic to a constitutional monarchy would certainly count as a move towards giving up on democracy, in Pettit's scheme. In order for the people to have control over their rule, which is what Pettit understands democracy to mean, they cannot be the subjects of an arbitrary ruler, no matter how tempered that subjection is by an elected parliament (Pettit, 2015: 6).

Gouges was not as committed to democracy as Pettit or we might be: for the thinkers of the French Revolution, democracy meant a small Athens-like government in which every decision was publicly debated and voted on. But she was committed to republican ideals of freedom as non-domination, and what she proposed in *Three Urns* could lead to a reinstatement of monarchic domination. So her proposal is significant: she thinks that bringing the monarchy back, and attempting to pursue republican values with that one very obvious obstacle, a non-elected monarch, would still be better for the people of France than being subjected to the arbitrary rule of Robespierre.

3.4 Liberty and Marriage

The final aspect of liberty defended by Gouges which I wish to address in this section relates to family law, and in particular divorce. In the Ancient Regime, a French marriage could only be annulled through a special dispensation from the Pope. In 1792, divorce became legal. A couple could now decide they simply no longer wanted to be married. In this case, they only had to wait six months after submitting a demand for divorce, and the divorce would be accepted after that period. Alternatively, one spouse could ask for divorce for reasons of cruelty, desertion, or infidelity, which was done through petition. From 1792 until the Napoleonic period, divorce was reasonably easy to obtain. Napoleon progressively made it harder, limiting acceptable reasons for divorce (Phillips, 1980: 58), and by 1816, when the monarchy was restored, divorce was no longer legal (Phillips, 1980: 213).

The first French divorce laws were drafted after 10 August 1792, when the republic was proclaimed. Divorce was very much on everybody's minds and had been since 1789 when the freeing of France from despotism was likened to the freeing of a woman from marriage to a tyrannical husband (Desan, 2004: 15). One defender of the Revolution, the Comte d'Antraigues, wrote that France, 'a nation for so long oppressed by despotism and its laws, all of a sudden becoming mistress of its own destiny, aspires for liberty' (Antraigues, 1789: 10–11). Sophie de Grouchy, who drafted her *Letters on Sympathy* in the early 1790s, also argued that divorce laws would, as part of general republican reforms, benefit French men and women and reduce crime – at least those crimes committed in the name of love (Grouchy, 2019: 140). Liberty, as trickled down to the people, was seen by all as affecting the family as much as the polis. Most of the French who had considered themselves oppressed had been oppressed in their daily lives, not their political participation, and unhappy marriages contributed a great deal to general unhappiness, judging by the number of divorce petitions that followed the new laws:

> What began as a trickle of divorce requests soon became a river, as family tribunals worked out interpretations of the new law. Remarking on this 'torrent' of divorces, the Journal et affiches du département de l'Oise commented in August 1793, 'You would think that a dam had been holding back all those who hoped to break their chains.' According to the best synthetic estimates, some 38,000 to 50,000 divorces took place during the eleven years from 1792 through 1803, when Napoleonic legislation restricted access to divorce. (Desan, 2004: 94)

From the beginning of the Revolution, then, the French saw strong connections between public and private liberty. As soon as the Revolution started, the public debate on marriage laws, which had already existed but had been constrained by the laws and the all-powerful clergy, suddenly amplified. Women's clubs throughout France discussed divorce, with the Cercle Social and its women-only offshoot, Le Club des Amies de la Verité, led by Etta Palm d'Aelders, spearheading the debate. Although some people still defended the indissolubility of marriage, at least in print, they were outnumbered by pro-divorce pamphlets and articles five to one (Desan, 2004:19).

Gouge's most publicly visible views on divorce were in the paragraph of the postscript of her *Declaration of the Rights of Woman*, which introduces her 'Frame for a Social Contract between Men and Women':

> Marriage is the tomb of trust and love. A married woman can, with impunity, give bastards to her husband and a fortune that is not theirs. The unmarried woman only has the feeblest rights; ancient and inhuman laws forbid her the right to the name or wealth of the father of her children, and no new laws have been devised to address this matter. If trying to give my sex an honourable and fair substance seems, at this time, paradoxical on my part, like attempting the impossible, then I will leave the glory of treating on this matter to the men to come but, while we wait, we can pave the way through national education, the reestablishment of morals, and by addressing conjugal conventions.
>
> (Gouges, 1791)

Her claim that marriage is 'the tomb of love' echoed that of the Comte d'Antraigues, who had compared the Revolution to a woman being finally free from her husband, and at the same time decried the laws that allowed parents to force marriage on their children: 'that sentiment and love are not even heard . . . it is not a marriage, it is a sacrifice, it is a sacrilege' (Antraigues, 1789: 23).

Previously, in her *Primitive Happiness* (1789) and a play entitled *The Necessity of Divorce* (1790b), Gouges had argued that marriage contracts should be based on love and trust, never imposed by others but freely chosen by both parties. In the passage quoted above, however, she highlights another problem arising from marriage laws: women, she says, only derive social status from their married state. That status is not substantial and allows women to live respectably in appearance while behaving immorally as long as they do not get caught. Unmarried women, on the other hand, have no status and no rights – they cannot even inherit their family's wealth. Reforming marriage laws and education at the same time (for she understands that laws alone won't do the job unless people are in a position at least to understand them) is the only way to help women regain some sort of 'substance'. So divorce was not only the means of preserving free relations between men and women, that is, relations without domination of one party by the other, but also a step towards establishing women as citizens on an equal footing with men.

The Necessity of Divorce, a play published in 1790, has more to say on how inflexible marriage laws can prevent a couple from living happily together. The play, set at the time it is written, depicts a young couple, Monsieur and Madame d'Aziuval, who married for love but are no longer happy together. Madame d'Aziuval is suspicious and jealous, and Monsieur d'Aziuval spends more and more time away from home, until he falls in love with a young woman who does not know he is already married. A close family friend, Rosambert, who has strong objections to marriage and believes that without the possibility of divorce married couples cannot be happy together, designs a plot to reconcile them. He announces to them (falsely) that the assembly has voted in favour of a divorce law:

> ROSAMBERT – Joy! Joy, my friends! You will be happy. The great decree is launched. The Assembly with one voice has pronounced in favour of divorce and you can finally break your irons. (Gouges, 1790b)

His announcement shocks the couple, who, confronted with the possibility of separation remember what they saw in each other when they chose to marry. They quickly reconcile, thereby proving Rosambert and Gouges's theory that marriages are stronger when divorce is possible.

Until it reaches this happy conclusion, the play describes the way in which bad marriages can destroy not only relationships but also individuals and how reasonable divorce laws are the only way to render relationships between men and women, parents and children, healthy. If a union is forced, either in choice or duration, affected parties will suffer psychologically. The force employed in keeping people together who wish to be apart, Gouges says, 'irritates and corrupts the human heart', but the possibility of divorce tempers this force and 'allows the knots of marriage to be tied with flowers, without it they become the irons that the trembling slave gnaws at for they are the torment of his life' (Gouges, 1790b).

The thought that marriage without divorce laws could lead to a tyrannical relationship is one that Gouges explores in the play through a character she clearly does not approve of, Father Basilie, an interfering Catholic priest who tries to persuade Madame d'Aziuval to cheat on her husband with him:

> Repeatedly exposed to the crude insults of a tyrant who treats you as a slave, who despises everything about you, who sees your qualities as defects or vices, subjected to duties that can sow in your bosom the fatal germ of a destructive poison, you cannot be blamed for refusing these tyrannical duties. (Gouges, 1790b)

Gouges would not deny that there is something tyrannical about the d'Aziuval marriage, but she thinks that both husband and wife act tyrannically towards each other, that each has trouble seeing in the other the qualities they fell in love with, that they feel the chains that force them to stay and pull on those of others at the same time. Marriage, Gouges says, has the capacity to make tyrants and slaves of both husband and wife at the same time, even when they love each other. Only the possibility of divorce can guarantee a free union that both parties can enjoy fully, without falling into a reciprocal relationship of tyrant and slave.

The argument Gouges attributes to Rosambert, and which she clearly shares, appeals to the Roman ideal of freedom as non-domination. Rosambert's reasoning links this ideal to arguments about virtue, which were central to the philosophy of the French Revolution. Without the possibility of divorce, marriage is merely a relationship of domination and cannot be happy because of the psychological effects of unfreedom upon the human mind. A dominated husband or wife cannot be a good partner, except through heroic effort on their part, because being dominated diminishes their capacity for virtue:

> Virtue enchained is a form of heroism that not everyone can attain. The perpetuity of marriage may have produced more horrors than the overreaching ambition of conquerors and the implacable cruelty of tyrants who swamped the earth in barbarian times. At least it was possible to flee their presence. No laws, raised to the level of dogma, forced people to await their blows. In an indissoluble marriage one must live with one's enemy, at times one's assassin, one must kiss the hand that will do harm and be caught between the cruel choice of living abjectly or dying unhappy.
>
> (Gouges, 1790b)

Thus, *The Necessity of Divorce* also has clear political implications. Free relationships, between ruler and ruled, superior and inferior, man and woman, were the first step to establish in order to build a republic after overthrowing tyranny: freedom is not the absence of rules, but rather learning to live together in freedom, without relying on mechanisms of domination which are also a great source of vicious behaviour by dominator and dominated both. Part of what was needed to establish relationships of freedom was a wider recognition of equality. This argument was a particularly powerful tool for understanding the position of women in society, as Mary Wollstonecraft also demonstrated two years later in her *Vindication of the Rights of Woman*. If women cannot be men's equal, she argued, then they are bound to hold back the progress of humanity (Wollstonecraft, 2014: 21, 22).[11]

4 Equality

We now turn to Gouges's arguments on equality. The idea, developed in the previous section, that liberty requires a certain maturity helps us understand the link between freedom and equality. When the revolution frees, it emancipates, and emancipation is often premised on a principle of equality – we are equal and equally deserve to become independent citizens. Thus, the debate on liberty in French revolutionary thought is intricately tied up with the debate on equality. For each class of people who need to acquire freedom, they must be

---

[11] For a discussion of Wollstonecraft's republicanism, see Coffee (2014) and Halldenius (2015).

emancipated from someone who is regarded as somehow superior to them and better suited to make decisions on their behalf. Therefore, a people must be shown to be equal to their king, a slave to their master, and women to men. Olympe de Gouges, defender of liberty, also argued for equality for all three groups. In the previous section, I explained how her arguments about liberty did the work of establishing a relation of equality between citizens and the state. In this section, I focus on what she had to say specifically about the equality of slaves and masters, and, with the exception of the debate on divorce, that of women and men.

The French Revolution from the start advocated equality and recorded it in the first efforts at drafting a constitution and a bill of rights. One of the writers of the Rights of Man and the Citizen, the Abbé Sieyès, had already voiced his commitment to equality in his influential pamphlet, written during the elections for the Estate Generals in 1788, *What is the Third Estate?*

> I picture the law at the center of an immense globe. All citizens without exception are at the same distance from it on the surface and occupy equal space. All equally depend on the law; all give it their liberty and property for protection. This is what I call the citizens' common right, whereby all are alike. . . . If . . . one person comes to dominate his neighbour, or to usurp his property, the common law will repress his attempt. (Sieyès, 2003: 156)

Sieyès's commitment to equality at that point seemed universal: "inequalities of sex, size, age, colour, etc. do not in any way denature civic equality" (Sieyès, 2003: 155). These, he said, like inequality of property, are incidental differences and cannot affect civic rights. Sieyès's 1789 proposal, however, did not result in the extending of rights to citizenship to women. Nor were his arguments sufficient to guarantee that Black men and women from the colonies who had been granted equality previously could retain their status, and certainly were not sufficient to free slaves. Because voting rights were also determined by tax brackets, half of France's white, male population were also passive citizens. Clearly, those most vulnerable were not going to benefit from this all-encompassing equality – the idea that citizens should participate equally in lawmaking was still a travesty. This was partly due to a distinction Sieyès himself made.

In an attempt to justify not granting the same rights to everyone, Sieyès drew a distinction between active and passive citizens. Active citizens were beneficiaries of political and social rights, passive citizens, of social rights only. Active citizens could participate in the running of the state. Passive citizens could not, but they were to have equal social rights to the active citizens. This meant that passive citizens could not vote, but they could, for instance, be granted divorce. They were persons in front of the law, not subsumed under someone else's rights:

> All of a country's inhabitants must enjoy the rights of passive citizenship: all
> have the right to the protection of their person, their property, their freedom,
> etc. But not all have the right to take an active part in the formation of public
> powers, all are not active citizens. Women, at least in the current state of
> things, children, foreigners, those that contribute nothing to supporting the
> public establishment must not actively influence the republic.
>
> (Sieyès, 1789: 14)

Women, free people of colour from the colony (slaves were not considered
citizens at all), and men who earned low wages would be passive citizens. In the
next subsections, I explore how Olympe de Gouges responded to the unjust
treatment of women and slaves.

4.1 Women

The distinction between active and passive citizenship and the exclusion of
entire groups of people from political participation did not go down well with
everyone. One objector was the philosopher Louise Kéralio-Robert, who wrote
in *Le Mercure National*, the newspaper she edited:

> We don't understand what [Sieyès] means when he says that not all citizens
> can take an active part in the formation of the active powers of the govern-
> ment, that women and children have no active influence on the polity.
> Certainly, women and children are not employed. But is this the only way
> of actively influencing the polity? The discourses, the sentiments, the prin-
> ciples engraved on the souls of children from their earliest youth, which it is
> women's lot to take care of, the influence which they transmit, in society,
> among their servants, their retainers, are these indifferent to the
> fatherland? . . . Oh! At such a time, let us avoid reducing anyone, no matter
> who they are, to a humiliating uselessness. (Kéralio, 1789)

Kéralio argued elsewhere for a firm distinction between men and women's
spheres of activity, saying that women ought to stay home as far as possible.
But she did not believe that this distinction was enough to discount the political
action women were capable of. She argued that women were politically influential from the home in that they were key in the development of the virtues of
citizenship, not only in their children but in everyone they interacted with,
including workers, tradespeople, and neighbours or visitors.

Olympe de Gouges certainly did not consider her citizenship to be 'passive'
but thought of herself as a major actor in revolutionary reforms. In her *Farewell
to Necker* (1790a) she wrote that she had become 'practically a man' through
her political activities, suggesting that she had taken on the role of active citizen
for herself. She had, after all, encouraged action that helped the country combat
poverty (with the voluntary tax) and advocated for several reforms that came to

pass (divorce and the abolition of slavery). And while she could not take part in the government, she regularly and publicly challenged its leaders.

But Gouges did not mean to set herself up as an exception, a 'femme forte' who could pretend to be a man in order to save the nation – following the example of Joan of Arc. She wanted all women to be considered full citizens. And to that effect, she published her *Declaration of the Rights of Woman* at the same time as the king was officially ratifying the Rights of Man and the new Constitution, which contained the distinction between active and passive citizens. Gouges's *Rights of Woman* included seventeen clauses mirroring those of the Rights of Man. The point was to show that women's need to be protected by rights was as important as men's. But there was more to it: Gouges also wanted to point to the shortcomings of a system of rights that saw the world only from the perspective of half its inhabitants. Human beings are not lone creatures, but they live and work together, with the heterosexual couple often central to communities. A list of rights of men *qua* individuals would not, Gouges suggested, capture the essence of human cooperation. This is particularly clear if we compare Articles III and IV of the Rights of Man and the *Rights of Woman*.

Article III of the Rights of Man states that sovereignty belongs to the nation. But the concept of a nation, of a people united by a culture and political interest, was fairly new in France, and some readers may well have wondered who, exactly, was the recipient of sovereignty. Article III of the *Rights of Woman* makes that clear by specifying that the nation consists of the 'union of man and woman'. Not only does this give some body to the idea of a nation, but it also offers an argument for the unity of the nation: it is like a marriage, a union that works through collaboration and that promotes the continuation of the human race. Gouges's reminder that individuals are already tied to each other through marriage and family makes it easier to understand what the nation might be, and whence its power may come. A family has a greater interest to serve than an individual – so does a nation.

Article IV of the Rights of Man states that liberty 'consists of doing anything which does not harm others: thus, the exercise of the natural rights of each man has only those borders which assure other members of the society the fruition of these same rights. These borders can be determined only by the law'. Gouges turns this around in article IV of the *Rights of Woman*: 'Liberty and justice exist to render unto others what is theirs; therefore the only limit to the exercise of the natural rights of woman is the perpetual tyranny that man opposes to it: these limits must be reformed by the laws of nature and reason.'

The idea behind the formulation of Article IV of the Rights of Man, that we are free as long as we do not harm others, is one that must appeal to a new liberated people who no longer have to fear the arbitrary rule of a tyrant. These newly liberated citizens must now learn not to harm others in order to protect their own liberty. If they do, all will be well. But Gouges points out that this is only true of (free) men. Women, who have not been granted the same rights, are still under the joug of the arbitrary rule of husband or father. A woman deciding how to act in such circumstances will not ask herself primarily whom her actions might harm, but whether she may act freely in the first place. She may even be questioning whether the idea of not stepping over one's borders into the domain of another is essential to defining liberty. As she showed in her third clause, liberty is best understood as relational; it is about how we treat the links that tie us to each other, not about how we avoid interfering with each other. Men and women are tied to each other, and freedom is not obtained by severing these ties to seek absolute independence but by removing any relation of domination from them. What her fourth clause achieves is to make it clear that Gouges's understanding of liberty in that sense is closer to the neo-Roman concept which French republicans adopted, while Article IV of the Rights of Man veers away from neo-Roman republicanism and towards liberalism. By the time the Napoleonic code was in place, it had become clear that 'man' stood for 'head of the family' and that very few questions could legitimately be asked about the relationships existing between family members. Gouges, by insisting on these relationships being the focus of freedom, is trying to ensure that women are not left out of the equation.

4.2 Slavery

While many writers and actors of the Revolution used the term slavery to describe the state of French citizens under monarchy, few were fully aware that the condition of actual enslaved people was distinct from that of subjects to the king, especially well-off subjects. Gouges was among these, and she made it her task to combat racial prejudice and make the conditions of life of enslaved people known to the general public.

At the time of the Revolution, slavery had been abolished on French territory. That meant that someone who had been enslaved who set foot in France was no longer a slave, and had to be let go or offered a wage. For some enslaved men and women this was not a real choice, as they would have nowhere to go should they leave their master's house.[12] There were also free people of African

---

[12] This was the case of Mary Prince, who came to England with the family which had bought her in 1828 and, upon finding out that she was legally free, was threatened with expulsion into the streets of London. 'This was the fourth time they had threatened turn me out, and, go where I might, I was determined now to take them at their word; though I thought it very hard, after I had lived with them for thirteen years, and worked for them like a horse, to be driven out in this

descent living in France, some of whom had either been enslaved or were descendants of people who had been. Some lived as peddlers in poverty, some were part of the servant and artisan classes, and some belonged to aristocratic colonial families who had come back to France.

People of mixed racial ancestry in the French colony were known as 'people of colour'. Those who had been free for several generations were sometimes very well off. Others were the issue of a white planter and a Black woman enslaved on their plantation, and if they were recognized by their father, would be accepted – in France, if not in the colonies – as belonging to the same social class as their fathers. One such person was the composer Joseph Bologne, Chevalier Saint Georges. Bologne was the stage manager for Madame de Maintesson's private theatre at the time Gouges was part of that group, and it is likely that they met there. But he was not the first 'person of colour' she had met, nor was he, according to her, the reason she became interested in the fate of slaves. In the addendum to the 1788 edition of her abolitionist play *Zamore et Mirza*, in a short essay entitled 'Réflexions sur les hommes nègres', she writes about her awakening to the absurdity of racial prejudice:

> As soon as I began to acquire some knowledge, and at an age where children do not yet think, the first sight of a negro woman led me to reflect and to ask questions about colour. Those I was able to interrogate then did not satisfy my curiosity nor my reason. They called these people brutes, creatures damned by God. But as I advanced in age, I saw clearly that it was force and prejudices that had condemned them to this horrible slavery, that Nature had no part in it, and the unjust and powerful interest of the Whites had done everything.
>
> (Gouges, 1788d)

She continues to argue that pro-slavery arguments suffer from a fundamental flaw: namely, that there are no natural differences between human beings based on their skin colour.

> A trade in men! . . . Almighty God! And Nature does not shudder! If they are animals, are we not likewise? How do Whites differ from this kind? It is in colour. . . .. Why does the pallid Blonde not want to cede to the Brunette who resembles a Mulatto? This impression is as striking as from the Negro to the Mulatto. The colour of mankind is nuanced, like all the animals that Nature has produced, as well as the plants and minerals. Why does day not compete with night or the sun with the moon and the stars of the firmament? All is varied, that is the beauty of Nature. Why then destroy her Work?
>
> (Gouges, 1788d)

---

way, like a beggar. My only fault was being sick, and therefore unable to please my mistress, who thought she never could get work enough out of her slaves; and I told them so: but they only abused me and drove me out. This took place from two to three months, I think, after we came to England' (Prince, 2006: 227).

Gouges was a little unusual – though by no means alone – in her fight against slavery. While the Roman republican rhetoric which defined liberty in opposition to slavery was popular among revolutionary politicians, not many were willing to consider the fate of enslaved Africans. When the Romans spoke of the evil of slavery, they most often did not mean that they thought there should be no slaves. The idea, instead, was that slavery was something to be avoided. To be free, in the Roman republican sense, literally meant not to be enslaved. But it could also be taken metaphorically: life under any kind of arbitrary power was, for the Romans, tantamount to slavery (*Digest*, 1985, I: 15). Quentin Skinner explained this as a way of defining slavery as 'belonging to someone else', being 'under someone else's rule', in someone else's sovereignty, and 'dependent on the good-will of someone else'. Recent neo-Roman republicans talk of liberty as non-domination or liberty as independence. To be free, they say, is not to depend on the good will of someone else (Skinner, 1998: 42).

Manon Roland, a contemporary of Gouges who moved in the same 'Girondin' circles and who was also very involved in the Revolution, was among those republican thinkers who used the Romans as a model for understanding liberty. But unlike Gouges, Roland did not seek to apply her anti-slavery rhetoric to what was happening in the colonies. Roland used the concept of slavery as a trope for defining liberty, one she applied to her republican critique of monarchy and of women's domination by men. She did denounce the actual practice of slavery in a 1777 essay, where she wrote that a republic is corrupt if it permits slavery and that the existence of the Helots in Sparta meant that the city-state failed to defeat the despotism they meant to combat: 'the rust of barbarity', she concludes, 'covers their proud masters and ruins them together. The poisoned breath of despotism destroys virtue in the bud' (Roland, 1864: 337).

Liberty, Roland argued, in agreement with Gouges, Brissot, and many other revolutionary republican thinkers, was guaranteed by virtue, and the loss of liberty in any part of the nation would mean corruption could set in:

> The rule of the general will is the only one that can maintain public happiness: from the moment power grants independence to some parts of the state [but not others], corruption is introduced and will manifest itself by enslaving the oppressed. (Roland, 1799–1800: 170)

Even when despotism is not actually active, the slightest deviation from the rule of the people, she says, could lead to enslavement. This is the converse of what she wrote in the 1777 essay, and it is clear that she believed both: corruption leads to slavery and slavery to corruption. Her enthusiasm for liberty, though, does not go beyond this, and any mention of slavery in her writing is usually metaphorical or referring to the condition of living under a despotic government. In one letter, published by Brissot in *Le Patriote Français* in April 1791, which she wrote standing during one of the sessions of the National Assembly, she announced the imminent enslavement of the French people:

> Throw your pen in the fire, o generous Brutus! And go cultivate your lettuces. For that is all that honest folk can do now. Unless a general insurrection saves us from death and slavery ... The Assembly is but the instrument of corruption and tyranny. (Roland, 1791)

Gouges, unlike Roland, openly condemned slavery and the slave trade. Her play *Zamore and Mirza, or the Lucky Shipwreck* argued that slavery was such a crime against human beings that it might even justify murder. Enslaved men and women, she showed in the play, were not only the equals of the planters who had bought them, in every natural quality, but because they were not the product of a corrupt system of education, they were usually morally superior to them. This echoes what we saw in Section 2, namely Gouges's belief that education can, if of the wrong sort, bring us so far from our nature that we are no longer capable of human happiness and virtue. In particular, excessive education is a bad thing because it creates a false sense of inequality.

In the passage below, the educated slave Zamore answers the question of his uneducated partner, Mirza, about what difference exists between planters and the men and women they enslave:

> This difference is a very insignificant thing; it exists only in colour, but the advantages that they have over us are immense. Skill put them above nature: instruction made Gods of them and we are mere mortals. They use us in these climes as they use animals in theirs. They came here, seized our land, our wealth, and enslaved us in recompense for the riches that they stole from us. The fields they reap are our very own, and the harvest is actually watered with our sweat and our tears. Most of these barbarous masters treat us with a cruelty that would make nature tremble; our too unhappy kind has become used to these chastisements. They carefully guard against instructing us; if our eyes were to open we would be horrified by the state to which they have reduced us and we could shake off a yoke that is as cruel as it is shameful.
> (Gouges, 1788d)

Gouges was harshly criticized for her condemnation of slavery: some planters, she claimed, even blamed her for the 1790 uprising in Haiti (Gouges, 1993: 136). She answered her critiques in two texts. The first was a *Letter to an American Planter* (1993), in which she argued that she did not incite revolt and that her writings were philanthropic and had justice on her side. She acknowledged that she prophesied the 1790 uprising, but stated that it was an 'invisible hand' that had started it and that she herself was blameless (Gouges, 1993: 137).

In the second text, the Preface to *L'esclavage des Noirs ou l'Heureux Naufrage*, the revised version of *Zamore and Mirza*, Gouges took a surprising turn and decided to admonish the men and women she had previously defended for taking the law in their own hands and starting a revolt (Gouges,1792e).

She tells the Haitian revolutionaries that they demonstrated by their 'ferocity and cruelty', that they truly belonged in chains. She argues that they ought to have waited for the law to change, for the French Revolution to do its work and abolish slavery. She adds that they already have more freedom than previously, and that in any case, they were better off as slaves in their colonies than in their native Africa, where she says they were hunted like animals by their own people.[13]

Truly shocked by the reports of violence she read, she nonetheless acknowledged that they were only hearsay – she had read reports from white men of crimes committed by Black men. She was inclined to believe these reports, no doubt, because she had witnessed similar crimes being committed in Paris by revolutionaries, and had been equally unimpressed.

What is particularly distinctive about Gouges's concept of equality is the way in which it interacts with her views on human nature and education. Others, though they were ready to assert that race or sex did not affect equality, found that education was nonetheless an obstacle in putting the belief that all humans are equal into practice. Sieyès argued, for instance, that women were not yet in a position to become active citizens. And although he does not specify outright that this was due to their lack of education, it seems as though the reason women, according to Sieyès, are not 'in the current state of things' in a position to participate in maintaining the public good is the fact that they are not as well educated as men (Sieyès, 1789: 14). One clue as to why this might be so is that Condorcet, in his argument for women being granted political rights, written a year after Sieyès's 'Préliminaire', argues that lack of education for some women is not a reason to exclude them from having full political rights. Some women, he says, are extremely well educated, while others who are not are quite capable of adapting their intelligence to political matters (Condorcet, 2012: 157, 159).

Similarly, Condorcet himself had argued that slavery could only be abolished slowly, over a period of seventy years, because those who were enslaved were not currently capable of enjoying their freedom. Slaves, he argued, were corrupted by their condition, they had become 'very stupid', which meant they were not fit to enjoy citizenship (Condorcet, 1822: 347).

---

[13] This was a common prejudice, fed by the fact that slavery did in fact exist in Africa, though it was greatly encouraged by white men's desire to purchase slaves.

Gouges, because she had very little trust in education, could argue that any human being, no matter what their level of education, could claim equal rights to any other. In fact, she appears to have thought that those who were currently enslaved were in a better position to contribute to politics than their masters, who no longer saw themselves as fully human. In this sense, her concept of equality had more potential for radical reform than either Condorcet or Sieyès.

5 Death, Reputation, and Legacy

5.1 Death

In July 1793, Olympe de Gouges was finally leaving Paris and its political feuds behind. She had threatened to retire or simply leave the country several times in the past few years. This time, she was committed: she had purchased a house in the country near Tours, near the home of her son's partner and their children, and she was looking forward to a peaceful life, at last.

A month earlier, Gouges had just visited her daughter-in-law and was probably already considering retirement when she returned to Paris. The day after her return, 2 June, the first decree against the Gironde was issued, Manon Roland was arrested, and several other Girondins, including Roland's husband and Brissot, had gone into hiding. Gouges then publicly took their defence: first she sent a note to the convention, in which she called its members 'blood-thirsty tigers' and 'avid monsters'. Then, understanding that she had already endangered her life, she prepared a pamphlet entitled *Political Testament*:

> If in a final effort, I can still save the Republic, I desire that even while they immolate me to their fury, my murderers should still envy my fate. And if one day, posterity notices women, perhaps the memory of my name will be of value. I have planned everything. I know that my death is unavoidable, but how beautiful and glorious it is, for a well-born soul, when ignominious death threatens all good citizens, still to give one's life for our dying country! (Gouges, 1793b)

At the beginning of July she returned to Tour and then purchased her retirement house, 'Le Clos-Figuier'. Back in Paris, she was busy packing her things and arranging for her furniture to be put in storage and removed to her new home. But she wasn't quite done yet with her political work. Her next tract, the 'Three Urns' (1793c), was an attack on the self-appointed leaders of the Paris Commune: Robespierre, Danton, and Marat. Like the Girondins whom she stood with, Gouges not only disliked the violence and bloodthirstiness of the members of the commune but was appalled by the fact that they had usurped the convention, with its deputies from all over France, and that it was now, in fact, Paris, not France, that governed. She responded to the Federalist riots that were happening throughout France by demanding that the French people be asked what they wanted, be it a republic, a federation, or a constitutional monarchy (Edmonds, 1983). She suggested that the commune itself, rather than helping France become a republic, was ruling as a tyrant. Louis XVI may be dead, she wrote, but he still reigned amongst them.

The tract was printed by her usual printer, Longuet, on 15 July. He drew 1,000 copies. Gouges dutifully sent a copy to the Committee of Public Safety and one to Hérault de Seychelle, responsible for the censorship of printed material. As no reply came she decided to go ahead and paste her pamphlet all over Paris. Her distributor, or *afficheur*, a Citizen Meunier, betrayed her when she brought him her pamphlet. First he refused to distribute her work on the grounds that he thought it would rain. Then he directed her to another distributor on the Pont Saint Michel. But he had her followed by his daughter and three members of the police. As soon as Gouges knocked at the door, Meunier's daughter pointed her out to three policemen and members of the national guard, who arrested her and dragged her to the Dépot prison of the City Hall. She was kept there in an isolated cell for several days. This was so that she could not warn her friend Michel de Cubière of her arrest. Cubière was secretary of the commune and had promised to help her if she was arrested. Unfortunately, by the time he found out, it was too late. On 28 July, she was taken to the Prison de l'Abbaye, which Manon Roland had left a month earlier for another prison, and where Brissot, the most famous of the Girondins, was still awaiting his trial.

Gouges was suffering from an injury to her knee that had become infected. At the end of August, four weeks after her arrest, she was transferred to La Petite Force, a prison which served as an infirmary, but which was also where the Princesse de Lamballe had been massacred in September 1792. La Petite Force was not, however, good enough as far as Gouges was concerned. In October, she pawned what she had left to pay for a private hospital-prison for male and female prisoners in the Chemin Vert, a long street on the Eastern edge of Paris, so named because of the vegetable gardens surrounding it. She stayed there till early November 1793, when she was brought to the Conciergerie, a medieval fortified prison on the Ile de la Cité, adjoining the Palais de la Justice. This was, for many Parisian prisoners, the last stop before the guillotine.

At her trial, Fouquier-Tinville, the public prosecutor, found her guilty of having produced a text in which she attacked the 'choice of the people', which was punishable by death. Gouges retorted that she could not be killed as she was pregnant:

> My enemies will not have the glory of seeing my blood flow. I am pregnant
> and will bear a *citoyen* or *citoyenne* for the Republic (Blanc, 2014: 220).

The law stated that she had to be examined by a medical team. Three health
inspectors and a midwife took her to the infirmary but could not draw any
conclusions: Gouges said she had been pregnant for five weeks only.

Fouquier-Tinville dismissed their hesitation and declared that her claim was
false:

> The Public Prosecutor notes that the accused was incarcerated for the past five
> months and that according to regulations, no contact was allowed between
> men and women in prisons. Therefore she made it up to avoid the death
> penalty. (Blanc, 2014: 222)

Fouquier-Tinville chose to ignore the fact that at the time she claimed she
became pregnant, Gouges had in fact been in a mixed private prison. On the
afternoon of 3 November 1793, Gouges was taken to the Place de la Revolution
and executed. Her last words were: 'Children of the Fatherland, you will avenge
my death!' (Blanc, 2014: 229).

5.2 Reputation

Olivier Blanc notes in the introduction to his biography of Gouges that historians of the eighteenth century have failed Gouges, as they have failed many
other significant women, and that she should long have been recognized for her
writings and her political activities. She is not well known, either as a political
philosopher or as a feminist. But why should we blame historians, rather than
the philosophers and feminist thinkers who have failed to turn to Gouges's large
output of writings in their work? Blanc's remark suggests, correctly, I think, that
a failure to acknowledge the historical significance of women of the past has
repercussions. Philosophers, when they turn to historical figures, rely on historians to guide them in their judgements as to the significance of historical figures.
Philosophers are not, on the whole, qualified to retrieve details about the
influence a particular author may have had during her lifetime on her contemporaries. But in the case of Olympe de Gouges, especially, historians have failed
us by focussing on inconsequential gossip instead of significant details about
her and her contribution to the politics and culture of her time.

While historians are generally careful when deciding on the reliability of their
sources when it comes to writing about men, their lives, their actions, and the
events that concerned them, the writing of women's lives by leading historians
still owes much to the techniques of the childhood game where one passes on
a whispered message to one's neighbour around a circle, until the original

message is unrecognizable. Here, too, rumours and gossip are copied from one inaccurate source to another until they find their place in respectable history books. One particular source for Gouges that is echoed in later records is the memoirs of the actor Fleury. In the second volume of his Memoires, the actor painted a long portrait of Gouges (Fleury, 1857: 85–105), where he describes her in turns as unfeminine (85), vain to excess (91), temperamental (102), untalented (85), cunning (103), holding ridiculous beliefs about animals (90), promiscuous (92), and more.

One notorious early twentieth-century biographer, Alfred Guillois, who presented his doctoral thesis on the topic of Olympe de Gouges and women's psychology during the French Revolution, made a note of all the rumours circulated about Gouges's promiscuity (Guillois, 1904: 19–20) and concluded that she made her money as a prostitute. We saw in Section 1 that she had in fact had an income settled on her by her lifelong partner, Biétrix de Rozières, to make up for the fact that they were not married and that he could not share his wealth with her as her husband. This was a perfectly respectable arrangement, and there is no evidence to suggest that Gouges obtained money or favours from any of the other men she was said to have taken as her lovers.

Perhaps Guillois did not have access to the archival materials Olivier Blanc studied to ascertain the source of Gouges's income. But Jonathan Israel, when he wrote *Revolutionary Ideas* (2014), did. Still, he refers to Olympe de Gouges as a prostitute ('high class courtisane', 123). Israel also falls for the old prejudice that women are particularly emotional creatures – Gouges is described as fiery (123), angry (122), and disgusted (400). And although her other political writings and activities are noted, it seems that Israel only considers her notable for her feminist writings, which means that the greatest part of her contributions to the ideas that shaped the Revolution are forgotten.

There are many (unreliable) precedents for Israel's description of Gouges as an emotional prostitute whose contributions to the Revolution concerned only the improvement of women's lot. One of them is Guillois (1904). Guillois was interested in the diseases of the mind and wanted to study the effect that the Revolution had on women's psychology, and especially how crowd psychology caused them to abandon their femininity. Unfortunately, he writes in his preface, he ran out of time and decided to focus on the mind of one particularly unfeminine woman, Olympe de Gouges. In his conclusion, he tells us that his findings, in fact, do apply to other women who participated in the Revolution – though there is no time to provide an actual argument for it.

Olympe de Gouges suffered from a delirium with systematizing tendencies which has been described by some authors as paranoid delirium (paranoia reformatoria). . . . She was predisposed to this, and the Revolution working on these prepared grounds found it easy to divert her from a normal mentality.

(Guillois, 1904: 87)

Guillois adds that her case is not isolated: 'we can say of numerous women who were active in the revolution and played a sanguinary role that they were unbalanced' (Guillois, 1904: 87). Guillois's very unpleasant comments on Gouges in particular and women of the Revolution more generally were in part motivated by a general conservative reaction to revolution at the end of the nineteenth century and beginning of the twentieth century in France. As a medical doctor, he would also have been influenced by the movement towards the medicalization of women, which aimed at treating women's attempts at participation, intellectual or political, as symptomatic (Theriot, 1993: 2).

Why does the misrepresentation of Gouges's life and character matter, as long as we get her philosophy right? It matters when the misrepresentations are such as to diminish our respect for the subject of biography. If Gouges was simply a loud and promiscuous opportunist, as Fleury would have it, or a woman suffering from serious mental health issues affecting her capacity for clear thought, as Guillois argues, then why should we take her seriously as a philosopher? Even John Cole, a sympathetic writer who dedicated an entire book to Gouges's *Rights of Woman*, was on the whole dismissive, claiming that 'Gouges was neither philosopher nor politician. She did not produce orderly arguments for women's rights, or against those who would deny them, and perhaps she could not have' (Cole, 2011: 5). On the question of whether her arguments were orderly, I hope I have shown not only that they were, but also that they were for the most part convincing and original, and that by studying them we can hope to gain a deeper understanding not only of feminism and abolitionism, but also of how the revolutionary ideals of liberty and equality contributed to the growth of republican and democratic ideals.

Cole attributes Gouges's significance, if not to her philosophical skills, to her 'boldness' in demanding equality for women (Cole, 2011: 5). He attributes her lack of success in persuading the authorities to listen to her having 'recklessly offended' her readers (8). What Cole's introduction tells us is that it is Gouges's character, rather than her arguments, that is worth studying. That, I contend, is the legacy of a historiography of rumour-mongering about women authors.

5.3 Legacy

One question that often comes up when assessing the legacy of women writers of the past who wrote about women's condition is whether it is at all right to call them feminists, or even proto-feminists. The main objection to doing so is that the word 'feminism' did not appear until the nineteenth century, so anyone before that could not have called themselves a feminist. This is, I find, a rather light objection. Coining a word is sometimes crucial for taking up a particular position, because it allows us to understand the situation we want to resist. For instance, Miranda Fricker has shown that there is a form of injustice pertaining to not having the concept to describe what is happening to us. For example, women who lost their jobs because they were sexually harassed at work, before that concept had been recognized and given a name, could not get organized to fight for their rights (Fricker, 2007: 149).

So is it an (epistemic) injustice to deny women of the past the label of 'feminism'? If it is, it is an injustice perpetrated against us, rather than them: by denying that there were feminists before the term was invented, we are failing to recognize the impact that women of the past and their struggles have had on our present condition, or, as Karen Offen put it, we are allowing the 'obliteration of an extraordinary struggle, one of continuing importance to women and men today' (Offen, 2000: 1).

Still, one might have qualms about using the word 'feminist' about an eighteenth-century writer because it is anachronistic, and anachronism ought to matter to historians. But this places unreasonable weight on the concept of linguistic anachronism. We are, after all, quite happy to talk about eighteenth-century salons to discuss literary or political gatherings in private homes, even though the term was not coined until the nineteenth century.[14] And, as Mary Garrard pointed out in a recent book on Italian painter Artemisia Gentileschi, we often use academic descriptions ana-chronistically without worrying that someone will think we are imputing anachronistic ideas to past thinkers:

> It is true that early modern pro-female and anti-misogynist writers were not called 'feminists' in their time. But, to repeat an analogy I have used before, the work of Galileo and Newton was not called science in their day; it was natural philosophy. Today they are regarded as founda-tional figures in the history of science – that is, scientists. Like science, feminism existed before we knew what to call it, and as with science, we must see the larger picture. If we do not recognize feminism as a continuum that has evolved over time, from the fourteenth century to the present, we risk separating women from our history and minimizing feminism's sig-nificance in history writ large. (Garrard, 2020: 9)

We do perhaps need to keep the vocabulary that Newton and Galileo and their contemporaries used to describe the work they did, at least in part because it allows us to see the metaphysical insights and methodological thoughts that shaped their

---

[14] I owe this excellent point to Severine Genièys-Kirk, in private correspondence.

discoveries about the world. But this does not affect their place in curricula or general culture. There are not courses on 'the history of natural philosophy' or 'natural philosophy' shelves in bookshops. Newton and Galileo can be found in the same courses and on the same shelves as Einstein or Marie Curie (although she might find her way on a 'women's studies' section). To insist that they are not to be studied as part of the history of science is pedantry, and the same is true of the claim that we should not see Gouges as a feminist.

Another objection to portraying Gouges as a feminist is that her struggle does not resemble ours. As Akkerman and Stuurman put it: past women's struggles 'evoke a mental universe and an intellectual context so different from ours that it cannot readily be located within the orbit of feminist discourse as we understand it' (Akkerman and Stuurman, 1998: 1). Akkerman and Stuurman's response to this lack of perfect fit is to propose a periodization of feminism, defining what it meant to be a feminist at a given period of history. They place Gouges in the Enlightenment feminism period. This, however, creates a problem in that they characterize that period as one where 'belief in reason shaped views of gender'. But while this is true of Wollstonecraft, we saw that it was less clearly the case for Gouges. Although she does enjoin women to hear the 'tocsin of reason resounding through the universe', she does not emphasize that it is because they are reasonable beings that men or women must have rights. Her emphasis, we saw, was on human beings' sociable and collaborative nature. But this need not be a decisive objection against classifying Gouges as an Enlightenment feminist. While in many ways she was an outlier of the Enlightenment, mostly because she did not rely on reason and education as much as her contemporaries did, she was also a product of it, influenced by Rousseau's political thought and by the emerging discourse of rights, liberty, and equality.

In order to argue that feminism was not born in the nineteenth century, Karen Offen (2000: 2) defines feminist struggles as 'political challenges and responses to male dominance and hegemony'. Akkerman and Stuurman offer a three-point definition:

1. the criticism of misogyny and male supremacy
2. the conviction that women's condition is not an immutable part of nature
3. a sense of group gender identity.

(Akkerman and Stuurman, 1998: 3–4)

It is clear that Gouges fits both definitions. Her *Rights of Woman* alone is evidence that she does. She asks men: 'What gave you the sovereign right to oppress my sex?' thereby criticizing (1) misogyny and male supremacy, and asserting (3) her identity as a member of the female sex. The first sentence of the postscript, where she enjoins women to 'wake up' and claim their rights, is recognition of (2): that women, as a group, have not yet understood their entitlement is explained by their having been asleep. While she does not put as much emphasis as her contemporaries on the need for education, she does believe that women's condition is in great part created by their indifferent upbringing, as she argues in the *Projet utile et salutaire* (2014: 23).

It is not much of a mystery why Gouges's importance as a feminist philosopher has not yet been recognized as it should; this is true of a great many women philosophers throughout history. While Mary Wollstonecraft's name is now frequently found in philosophical articles and syllabi, this was not the case ten years ago. But Wollstonecraft was already well known in academic circles, though mostly gender study, history, and literature. Gouges, it seems, hasn't yet been admitted to these research networks to the extent that Wollstonecraft had a decade ago. This is in part due to the fact that her works – like many texts written during the French Revolution – are hard to find. It is to be hoped that the digitization of her pamphlets by the French National Library (BNF and Gallica) will help facilitate the spread of her work and the willingness to treat it as a serious contribution to the political philosophy of the French Revolutionary period.

Olympe de Gouges's legacy, whether as a feminist or simply a political philosopher, has not been recognized as it should. This is true outside of academia as well: in France, there are few odonymical marks of her existence. Some French public building and streets have been named after Olympe de Gouges, including the Place Olympe de Gouges in the 3rd Arrondissement in Paris, a gynaecological and maternity health centre in Tours, a theatre in her native Montauban, and most recently a lecture theatre in Bordeaux. But the number of places and institutions named for Gouges represents a very small percentage of the primary schools named after, for instance, nineteenth-century historian Jules Michelet.

In 2014, Gouges was brought to the political limelight when feminist historian Eliane Viennot addressed the French National Assembly on the need to reform the most gendered aspects of the French language. Viennot argued that the call to reform the French language to include women as equals dates back to the Revolution, and in particular to Gouges's *Declaration of the Rights of Woman*, which was a direct challenge to the failure to include women in the new Constitution. Viennot has since been involved in the controversy over 'inclusive writing', or the move to reform the grammatical law which claims that the masculine is always stronger than the feminine, and in that work, too, Viennot claims the influence of Gouges (Develey, 2017).

Although Gouges has been a candidate for entry in the Paris Panthéon, where the ashes of 'great men of France' are interred (or where their names are recorded where there were no remains to be found), she has not yet been successful. Were she to enter this hallowed place, she would be reunited with some friends and enemies: Mirabeau and Marat were interred at their death, Rousseau was transferred there in 1794, and Grégoire and Condorcet were transferred in 1789, on the bicentenary of the French Revolution. As a philosopher of the French Revolution who produced over a hundred texts in a six-year period, who defended women's rights and abolitionism, and who opposed the extremist practices of Robespierre, we should treat her as a pioneer of political thought, one we can still learn from.

References

Akkerman, T., and Stuurman, S. (1998). Perspectives on Feminist Political Thought in European History: From the Middle Ages to the Present. London; New York: Routledge.

Antraigues, E.-H.-L. (1789). Observations sur le divorce. Paris: Imprimerie nationale.

Bergès, S. (2015). Sophie de Grouchy and the Cost of Domination in *The Letters on Sympathy* and Two Anonymous Articles in *Le Républicain*. The Monist, 98 (1), 102–12.

Bergès, S. (2018). Olympe de Gouges versus Rousseau: Happiness, Primitive Societies, and the Theater. Journal of the American Philosophical Association 4 (4), 433–51.

(2019a). Revolution and Republicanism: Women Political Philosophers of Late Eighteenth-Century France and Why They Matter. Australasian Philosophical Review 3 (4), 351–70.

(2019b). Wollstonecraft. In G. Oppy, ed., A Companion to Atheism and Philosophy. Oxford: Wiley-Blackwell, pp. 58–70.

Blanc, O. (2014). Olympe de Gouges: Des droits de la femme à la guillotine. Paris: Tallandier.

Brissot, J.-P. (1791). Nouveau voyage dans les Etats-Unis de l'Amérique Septemtrionale, fait en 1788, par J.P. Brissot (Warville) Citoyen François 1791. Paris: Chez Buisson.

Burke, E. (1986). Reflections on the Revolution in France. Harmondsworth: Penguin.

Coffee, A. (2014). Freedom As Independence: Mary Wollstonecraft and the Grand Blessing of Life. Hypatia 29 (4), 908–24.

Cole, J. R. (2011). Between the Queen and the Cabby. Montreal: McGill-Queen's University Press.

Condorcet, N. (1822). Esquisse d'un tableau des progrès de l'esprit humain; suivi de réflexions sur l'esclavage des nègres, par Condorcet. Paris: Masson et Fils.

(2012). Political Writings. Edited by Steven Lukes and Nadia Urbinati. Cambridge: Cambridge University Press.

Condorcet, N., and Paine, T. (1991). Aux origines de la république 1789–1792, Vol. 3: Le républicain par Condorcet et Thomas Paine, 1791. Paris: EDHIS.

D'Alembert, J. R. (1757). Genève. In D. Diderot, ed., Encyclopédie ou Dictionnaire Raisonné des Sciences, des Arts et des Métiers, Vol. 7. Paris: André le Breton, 1751–66, pp. 578–578D.

Desan, S. (2004). The Family on Trial in Revolutionary France. Berkeley: University of California Press.

Develey, A. (2017). Éliane Viennot: 'Olympe de Gouges a lancé les prémices de l'écriture inclusive'. Le Figaro, 5 November. https://bit.ly/3sc6wHf.

Dumont, E. (1832). Souvenirs sur Mirabeau et sur les deux premières assemblées législatives. Paris: Librairie de Charles Gosselin.

Edmonds, B. (1983). 'Federalism' and Urban Revolt in France in 1793. The Journal of Modern History 55 (1), 22–53.

Fleury. (1857). Mémoires de Fleury de la comédie française, Vol. 2: 1789–1820. Paris: Lafitte.

Fricker, M. (2007). Epistemic Injustice: Power and the Ethics of Knowing. Oxford: Oxford University Press.

Garrard, M. D. (2020). Artemisia Gentileschi and Feminism in Early Modern Europe. London: Reaktion Books.

Gouges, O. (1786). *L'homme généreux* [The Generous Man]. Translated by Clarissa Palmer. www.olympedegouges.eu/homme_gen.php.

(1788a). Madame de Valmont, preface pour les dames. In Oeuvres de Madame de Gouges, dediées à Monseigneur Le Duc D'Orleans. Paris: L'Autheur. http://gallica.bnf.fr/ark:/12148/bpt6k6546469r.r=gouges.

(1788b). Lettre au people ou projet d'une caisse patriotique [Letter to the People, or Patriotic Purse Project]. Translated by Clarissa Palmer. www .olympedegouges.eu/patriotic_purse.php.

(1788c). Remarques patriotiques. Patriotic Observations. Translated by Clarissa Palmer. www.olympedegouges.eu/patriotic_observations.php.

(1788d). Réflexions sur les hommes nègres, *Zamore et Mirza ou l'heureux naufrage, drame Indien* [Reflections concerning Black Men, Zamore and Mirza, or the Fortunate Shipwreck, an Indian drama]. Translated by Clarissa Palmer. www.olympedegouges.eu/zamore_et_mirza.php.

(1789). Le bonheur primitif, ou rêveries patriotiques. Amsterdam and Paris: Royer. https://bit.ly/34thjEJ.

(1790a). Depart De M. Necker Et De Madame De Gouges, ou les adieus de Madame De Gouges aux Français et A M. Necker [M. Necker and Madame de Gouges's Departure or Madame de Gouges's Farewells to the French and to M. Necker]. Translated by Clarissa Palmer. www .olympedegouges.eu/departdenecker.php.

(1790b). La nécéssité du divorce [The Necessity of Divorce]. Translated by Clarissa Palmer. www.olympedegouges.eu/le_divorce.php.

(1791). Les droits de la femme, A la reine [The Rights of Woman, to the Queen]. www.olympedegouges.eu/rights_of_women.php.

(1792a). Le bons sens Français ou l'apologie des vrais nobles, dédiée aux Jacobins [French Commonsense or the Vindication of True Nobles, Dedicated to the Jacobins]. Translated by Clarissa Palmer. www .olympedegouges.eu/french_commonsense_nobles.php.

(1792b). Les fantomes de l'opinion publique [The Ghosts of Public Opinion]. www.olympedegouges.eu/ghost.php.

(1792c). Réponse à la justification de Maximilien Robespierre, adressée à Jérôme Pétion, par Olympe de Gouges [Response to Maximilien Robespierre's Justification, Addressed to Jérôme Pétion, by Olympe de Gouges]. Translated by Clarissa Palmer. www.olympedegouges.eu/response_max.php.

(1792d). Olympe de Gouges, défenseur officieux de Louis Capet [Olympe de Gouges, Louis Capet's Unofficial Advocate]. Translated by Clarissa Palmer. www.olympedegouges.eu/defenseur_officieux.php.

(1792e). L'esclavage des noirs ou l'heureux naufrage, drame en trois actes. Représenté à la comédie française en Décembre 1789. Paris. http://gallica .bnf.fr/ark:/12148/bpt6k566870.

(1793a). Arrêt de mort que présente Olympe de Gouges contre Louis Capet [Decree of Death against Louis Capet, presented by Olympe de Gouges]. Translated by Clarissa Palmer. www.olympedegouges.eu/decree_of_death .php.

(1793b). Testament politique d'Olympe de Gouges [Olympe de Gouges's Political Statement]. Translated by Clarissa Palmer. www.olympedegouges .eu/political_testament.php.

(1793c). Les trois urnes [The Three Urns]. Translated by Clarissa Palmer. www.olympedegouges.eu/three_urns.php.

(1993). Olympe de Gouges: Écrits politiques (1789–1791). Vol. 1, Réponse au champion américain, préface d'Olivier Blanc. Coll. 'Des femmes dans l'histoire'. Paris: Côté-femmes Éditions.

(2014). Projet utile et salutaire. In Femme reveille-toi! Déclaration des droits de la femme et de la citoyenne et autres écrits. Edited by Martine Reid. Paris: Gallimard, pp. 18–29.

Green, K. (2014). A History of Women's Political Thought in Europe, 1700–1800. Cambridge: Cambridge University Press.

Grouchy, S. (2019). Sophie de Grouchy's Letters on Sympathy. Translated by Sandrine Bergès. Edited by Sandrine Bergès and Eric Schliesser. New York: Oxford University Press.

Guillois, A. (1904). Thesis presented and passed on 12 December 1904 on Olympe de Gouges, considerations generals sur la mentalité des femmes pendant la revolution. Lyon: Faculty of Medicine and Pharmacy. Lyon: A. Rey, Imprimeur-Editeur de l'Université.

Halldenius, L. (2015). Mary Wollstonecraft and Feminist Republicanism. London: Pickering & Chatto.

Harth, E. (1992). Cartesian Women. Ithaca, NY: Cornell University Press.

Hobbes, T. (1986). Leviathan. Edited by C. B. MacPherson. London: Penguin.

Hont, I. (2005). Jealousy of Trade. Cambridge, MA: Harvard University Press.

Israel, J. (2014) Revolutionary Ideas: An Intellectual History of the French Revolution from The Rights of Man to Robespierre. Princeton, NJ: Princeton University Press.

Kant, I. (1991). An Answer to the Question What Is Enlightenment. In Political Writings. Edited by H. S. Reiss. Cambridge: Cambridge University Press.

Kéralio L. (1789). Article in Le Mercure National ou Journal d'État et du citoyen, 20 August. Par Mademoiselle de Keralio & MM. Carra, Masclet et Hugou de Bassville.

Linton, M. (2013). Choosing Terror: Virtue, Friendship, and Authenticity in the French Revolution. Oxford: Oxford University Press.

Macaulay, C. (1790) Letters on Education: With Observations on Religious and Metaphysical Subjects. London: C. Dilly.

Momsen, T., Krueger, P., and Watson, A. (1985). The Digest of Justinian, 4 Vols. Philadelphia: University of Pennsylvania Press.

Monnier R. (1999). Démocratie et révolution française. In: Mots, 59, juin 1999, 47–68.

Mousset. S. (2007). Women's Rights and the French Revolution: A Biography of Olympe de Gouges. Translated by Joy Poirel. New Brunswick, NJ: Transaction Publishers.

Offen, K. (2000). European Feminisms, 1700-1950: A Political History. Stanford, CA: Stanford University Press

Pateman, C. (1980). 'The Disorder of Women': Women, Love and the Sense of Justice. Ethics, 91 (1), 20–34.

Pettit. P. (2012). On the People's Terms. Cambridge: Cambridge University Press.

(2015). Three Mistakes about Democracy. Kilikya Felsefe Dergisi, 2 (2), 1–15.

Phillips, R. (1980). Family Breakdown in Late Eighteenth-Century France. Oxford: Clarendon Press.

Prince, M. (2006). The History of Mary Prince, a West Indian Slave, Related by Herself. In Broadview Anthology of British Literature, The Concise Edition, Vol. B. Peterborough: Broadview Press, pp. 263–90.

Ramgotra, M. (2014). Conservative Roots of Republicanism. Theoria: A Journal of Social and Political Theory, 61 (139), 22–49.

Reuter, M. (2019). Equality and Difference in Olympe de Gouges' Les droits de la femme. A La Reine. Australasian Philosophical Review, 3 (4), 403–12.

Robespierre, M. (1792). Speech reported in Gazette Nationale ou Moniteur Universel, 6 November 1792, Convention Nationale, Séance du 5 Novembre.

Roland, M.-J. (1791). Letter to Brissot, 28 April 1791, edited by Brissot and published in the Patriote Français on 30 April 1791.

(1799–1800). Œuvres de J. M. Ph. Roland, femme de l'ex ministre de l'intérieur. Vol. III. Edited by L. A. Champagneux. Paris: Bidault.

(1827). Mémoires de Madame Roland, avec une notice sur sa vie, des notes et des éclaircissements historiques, Vol. I, 3rd ed. Edited by Saint-Aubin Berville and Jean-François Barrière. Paris: Baudoin Frères.

(1864). Mémoires de Madame Roland. New edition, Vol. II. Edited by François Alphonse Faugères. Paris: Hachette.

(1902). Mémoires de Madame Roland. Perroud, Vol 1. Paris: Plon.

Roubaud, Abbé. (1786). Nouveaux synonymes françois. Vol. 2. Liège: Plomteux.

Rousseau, J.-J. (1997) *The Discourses and Other Early Political Writings*. Edited by Victor Gourevitch. Cambridge: Cambridge University Press.

(1968). Letter to D'Alembert on the Theatre. In Politics and the Arts. Translated by Allan Bloom. Ithaca, NY: Cornell University Press.

(1979). Emile, or on Education. Translated by Allan Bloom. New York: Basic Books.

Saint-Pierre, J.-H.-B. (1836). Vœux pour une éducation nationale. In Oeuvres de Jacques-Henri-Bernardin de Saint-Pierre, Vol. 11. Edited by L. Aimé-Martin. Paris: chez Méquignon-Marvis, libraire.

Scott, J. (1997). Only Paradoxes to Offer: French Feminists and the Rights of Man. Boston, MA: Harvard University Press.

Scurr, R. (2013). Varieties of Democracy in the French Revolution. In Joanna Innes and Mark Philp, eds., Re-imagining Democracy in the Age of Revolutions: America, France, Britain, Ireland 1750–1850. Oxford: Oxford University Press, pp. 57–68.

Sherman, C. L. (2013). Reading Olympe de Gouges. New York: Palgrave Macmillan US.

Sieyès, E. J. (1789). Préliminaire de la Constitution. Versailles: Imprimerie Pierre.

(2003). What is the Third Estate? In Political Writings, including the Debate between Sieyès and Tom Paine 1791. Translated and edited by Michael Sonenscher. Indianapolis: Hackett.

Skinner, Q. (1998). Liberty before Liberalism., Cambridge: Cambridge University Press.

Smart, A. (2011). Citoyennes: Women and the Ideal of Citizenship in Eighteenth-Century France. Newark: University of Delaware Press.

Theriot, N. M. (1993). Women's Voices in Nineteenth-Century Medical Discourse: A Step toward Deconstructing Science. *Signs* 19 (1), 1–31.

Trouille, M. S. (1997). Sexual Politics in the Enlightenment. Albany, NY: SUNY Press.

Wollstonecraft, M. (2014). A Vindication of the Rights of Woman. Edited by Eileen Hunt Botting. New Haven, CT: Yale University Press.

Cambridge Elements ≡

Women in the History of Philosophy

Jacqueline Broad

Monash University

Jacqueline Broad is Associate Professor of Philosophy at Monash University, Australia. Her area of expertise is early modern philosophy, with a special focus on seventeenth and eighteenth-century women philosophers. She is the author of *Women Philosophers of the Seventeenth Century* (CUP, 2002), *A History of Women's Political Thought in Europe, 1400–1700* (with Karen Green; CUP, 2009), and *The Philosophy of Mary Astell: An Early Modern Theory of Virtue* (OUP, 2015).

Advisory Board

Dirk Baltzly, *University of Tasmania*
Sandrine Bergès, *Bilkent University*
Marguerite Deslauriers, *McGill University*
Karen Green, *University of Melbourne*
Lisa Shapiro, *Simon Fraser University*
Emily Thomas, *Durham University*

About the Series

In this Cambridge Elements series, distinguished authors provide concise and structured introductions to a comprehensive range of prominent and lesser-known figures in the history of women's philosophical endeavour, from ancient times to the present day.

Cambridge Elements

Women in the History of Philosophy

Elements in the Series

Pythagorean Women
Caterina Pellò

Frances Power Cobbe
Alison Stone

Olympe de Gouges
Sandrine Bergès

A full series listing is available at: www.cambridge.org/EWHP

Printed in the United States
by Baker & Taylor Publisher Services